"Veteran professor of theology, participant in several national ecumenical conversations, and responsive to both the academic and pastoral needs of his students, Thomas Rausch brings several important issues to the fore in this book. After providing a history of the Jesuit involvement in higher education, he critically examines recent studies on how young people today relate to the Church and religion in general. While that situation is cause for real concern, Rausch includes in his book five chapters by other authors who describe effective ways to bring college-age youth to a deeper understanding and love of their faith. In the last chapter, drawing on his own wide experience and pastoral wisdom, Rausch suggests what can and should be done today to pass on the faith to the next generation. I highly recommend the book for anyone concerned about youth and the future of the Church."

> —Fr. James L. Heft, SM
> Alton Brooks Professor of Religion
> President: Institute for Advanced Catholic Studies
> University of Southern California, Los Angeles

"Thomas Rausch has done a notable service for those concerned with furthering the Catholic nature of higher education today. Rausch has earlier written about the difficulties of maintaining a vigorous Catholic identity in a culture of choice which prioritizes pluralism. He wrestles and imagines ways to improve Catholic identity at Catholic universities which share that culture of choice and pluralism. Helpful chapters deal with Catholic Studies programs, faith and justice insertion programs, and pilgrimage retreats. This is a book not only for those interested in improving the Catholic character of Catholic universities but also for anyone concerned about the faith future for young adult Catholics."

> —John A. Coleman, SJ
> Associate pastor at Saint Ignatius Church, San Francisco
> Previous Charles Casassa Professor of Social Values at Loyola
> Marymount University, Los Angeles

Educating for Faith and Justice

Catholic Higher Education Today

Thomas P. Rausch, S.J.

A Michael Glazier Book

LITURGICAL PRESS
Collegeville, Minnesota

www.litpress.org

A Michael Glazier Book published by Liturgical Press

Cover design by Ann Blattner. Photo by Michael Crouser.

1   2   3   4   5   6   7   8   9

Library of Congress Cataloging-in-Publication Data

Rausch, Thomas P.
    Educating for faith and justice : Catholic higher education today / Thomas P. Rausch.
      p. cm.
    "A Michael Glazier book."
    Includes index.
    ISBN 978-0-8146-5459-0
    1. Catholic universities and colleges—United States.   2. Catholic Church—Education.—United States.   I. Title.
    BX922.R38   2010
    378.0088'28273—dc22   2009038975

For my Jesuit brothers

Contents

Acknowledgments   ix

Introduction   xi

1. Catholic Colleges and Universities in the United States   1
Jesuit Colleges   3
Catholic Higher Education in the United States   12
Conclusion   18

2. Theology and the University   20
The Magisterium of the Doctors   21
From Christian Wisdom to Critical Discipline   23
From Clerical to Lay Profession   27
Undergraduate Theology Today   32
Conclusion   37

3. Education for Faith and Justice   39
The Church in the Modern World   39
Pedro Arrupe   43
Proyección Social   47
Conclusion   55

4. Young Adult Catholics Today   58
The Data   59
Some Initial Reflections   64
Strategies   66
Conclusion   73

5. Catholic Studies, *Don J. Briel*   76
Catholic Studies Programs   78
The Center for Catholic Studies   86
Conclusion   90

6. A Pilgrimage to Rome, *David Gentry-Akin* 92
Walking in the Footsteps of the Early Christians 94
Processing the Experience 99
Conclusion 101

7. Community-Based Learning, *Kristin E. Heyer* 103
Transformative Pedagogy in Christian Ethics 104
Moving Beyond the Confines of Coursework 107
Conclusion 109

8. Praxis-Based Education, *Mark Ravizza, S.J.* 111
Academic Reflection Rooted in Reality 113
Integrated Community Learning 116
Recollection and Pedagogical Accompaniment 118
Formation of a Christic Imagination 123
Conclusion 125

9. Immersion Trips, *Stephen J. Pope* 127
Why Spend Money to Visit Poor People in Another Country? 130
Levels of Personal Transformation 133
Conclusion 141

10. Meeting the Living God 143
Spirituality, not Religion 144
Faith without Accountability 145
Counter Voices 148
Beyond a Culturally Determined Faith 151
Conclusion 154

Contributors 157

Index 159

Acknowledgments

I would like to acknowledge several friends who got me thinking about this book. They include Michael Glazier, an old friend whose interest has inspired a number of my books; Michael Engh, S.J., then my dean, now president of Santa Clara University; and Jeffrey Siker, my chair here at Loyola Marymount.

Two of the chapters were originally given for the Catholics on Call Partners' Conference at the Chicago Theological Union in September of 2008. I am grateful to Robin Ryan, C.P., who invited me to be the keynote speaker. An earlier version of Don J. Briel's chapter was published in *Catholic Education*, March 2009. I am especially grateful to Robert Lassalle-Klein for his help in developing the section on Ignacio Ellacuría, to my colleagues Don Briel, David Gentry-Akin, Kristin Heyer, Stephen J. Pope, and Mark Ravizza, S.J., for their fine contributions, and to Mary Stommes of Liturgical Press for her careful copyediting.

Thomas P. Rausch, S.J.

Introduction

Religious education has always been a priority in the Catholic Church, particularly in the United States, with its extensive system of primary and secondary schools as well as its network of some 235 colleges and universities. And while from one perspective, the goals and methods of religious education have changed little over the years, from another, the field is very much alive, with new approaches to pedagogy, formation, and school organization. New initiatives include faith-based Nativity schools for sixth to eighth graders, the Christo Rey network of high schools, and a new emphasis on education for justice, service or community based learning, learning communities, and immersion trips in Catholic colleges and universities.

Nativity schools, now called NativityMiguel schools, are designed to support and help motivate inner-city students who so often are not well served by the public school system. They provide a longer, highly structured day, generally three hours more than in other schools, smaller classes, and a personal care, with the goal of preparing these students for college. The first Nativity school was established by the Jesuits in 1971 on Manhattan's lower East Side for low, income Hispanic boys. Today there is a network of some sixty-four NativityMiguel schools, so-called after a similar program developed by the Christian brothers was merged with the Nativity schools.[1] The Jesuits run sixteen, while the rest are administered by other Catholic religious men and women as well as by some Episcopalians and Lutherans.

The Cristo Rey network developed from a Jesuit initiative for inner-city students in Chicago in 2001. Designed to prepare these students for college, it incorporates a work-study model which places students in professional jobs five days a month, both to give them professional work experience and to help defer the cost of their education. There are some twenty-two schools in the Cristo Rey network in nineteen urban centers across the country, and

---

1. See www.nativitymiguelschools.org.

more are being planned. The majority of their students, 95 percent, are from minority communities. In 2008, 99 percent of their graduates were accepted by two- or four-year colleges.[2]

Theological education in Catholic colleges and universities in the United States has also seen considerable change, from its early days when all students took a virtual minor in "religion" to the current diminished place of theology or religious studies in the curriculum. At a time when a number of studies and commentators are calling attention to theological illiteracy and lack of familiarity with the Catholic tradition which affects so many young Catholics today,[3] I want to focus in this study on the place of theology in Catholic higher education.

The first chapter focuses on Catholic higher education in the United States in general. It begins with the Jesuits, who as the first teaching order in the church were the first to establish an international network of schools, grounded in a common philosophy of education, and they continue to play an important role in Catholic higher education today. But our concern is considerably broader. The chapter also surveys how Catholic higher education in the United States changed in the late nineteenth and early twentieth centuries, from colleges combining secondary and baccalaureate studies on the European model to institutions like their American counterparts. As these schools went through a process of professionalization, particularly in the period after Vatican II, increasing the number of lay professors, adding graduate programs, rethinking their curricula, reducing the emphasis on philosophy and Catholic theology that had once been central, new questions about their Catholic identity began to surface that are still with us today.

Chapter 2 explores the place of theology in the university, from the role theologians played in the great universities of the Middle Ages to the gradual transformation of theology from a Christian wisdom into a critical discipline. The further development of Catholic theology in the twentieth century has raised new questions about its relation to the church and the nature of the discipline itself in Catholic institutions which at the same time have become increasingly pluralistic in terms of both their faculties and their student bodies.

Chapter 3 surveys the turn towards what is often called the faith that does justice which emerged after Vatican II. The Council moved the church from

2. See http://www.cristoreynetwork.org/; also G. R. Kearney, *More than a Dream: The Cristo Rey School: How One School's Vision Is Changing the World* (Chicago: Loyola Press, 2008).

3. See Thomas P. Rausch, *Being Catholic in a Culture of Choice* (Collegeville, MN: Liturgical Press, 2006) 16–18.

its defensive position over against the world to a new one that saw itself at the world's service, particularly the service of the poor and the disadvantaged. The result was a new emphasis on social justice, illustrated here by the leadership of Jesuit Father General Pedro Arrupe, by the Jesuits of the University of Central America in El Salvador, as well as by the increasing prominence of experiential or praxis-based learning in Catholic colleges and universities in the United States.

Chapter 4 seeks to know more fully the young men and women who come to these colleges and universities today. A number of recent surveys raise serious questions about their Catholic identity and commitment to the institutional church. Several other sources, more encouraging, stress the degree to which young Catholics have interiorized the teachings of the council, bring their own critical questions to the tradition, and are interested in ministry.

The next five chapters explore a number of new initiatives in Catholic higher education and theology, engaging the intellectual and cultural depths of the Catholic tradition and moving towards a more experience-based approach to theology that opens students to the broader world beyond the classroom and especially to the poor in their real-life situations. The programs, methods, and approaches outlined in these chapters, whether for service learning courses, new departments like Catholic Studies, interterm, alternative spring break, or term-long study abroad courses, show great promise for deepening and making more explicit the religious identity of Catholic colleges and universities. It is encouraging to gain a sense for how much has already been done.

Chapter 5, by Don J. Briel, director of the Center for Catholic Studies at the University of St. Thomas in St. Paul, Minnesota, reviews the development of Catholic studies programs, with an emphasis on interdisciplinary courses that engage the university as a whole. His chapter introduces new initiatives and programs that broaden the educational experience of the students and serve to renew the institution's Catholic identity.

Chapter 6, by David Gentry-Akin of Saint Mary's College of California, outlines an interterm course for students designed as a pilgrimage that combines prayer and liturgy with studying and visiting historic Christian sites in Rome, making it possible for them to "walk in the footsteps of the early Christians." It is part of a program at Saint Mary's that offers students various study abroad courses and immersion experiences.

Chapter 7, by Kristin Heyer of Santa Clara University, explores community-based learning as a practical way of letting "the gritty reality of this world into the students' lives" and challenging their unexamined assumptions. Professor Heyer has developed a number of community-based learning courses, on Catholic social teaching and action, on Christian ethics and social responsibility, and a particularly effective one on Christian ethics and HIV/AIDS. Her courses include a final practical integration project that challenges students to apply what they have learned.

Chapter 8, by Mark Ravizza, S.J., also from Santa Clara University, roots an emphasis on praxis-based education in the writings of Jesuit Father General Peter-Hans Kolvenbach. He focuses on a course he has taught at the *Casa de la Solidaridad* in El Salvador that combines immersion in the lives of the poor with rigorous academic study. Drawing on the written reflections of his students, he shows how they moved beyond preconceived ideas and the easy answers of their unexamined faith in the direction of what William Lynch has called a "Christic" imagination.

Chapter 9, by Stephen Pope of Boston College, describes an immersion trip to El Salvador. Addressing specifically the often heard objection—why spend money to visit the poor in another country when there are plenty of them here at home?—he shows how even relatively brief immersion trips, for example, during a spring break, can facilitate the personal transformation of students on social, moral, and spiritual levels. They return with real questions which arise out of their lived experience.

The final chapter raises the question, how can we help our students come to a personal encounter with the divine mystery revealed in Jesus? Critiquing the current efforts to uncouple spirituality from religion and the tendency to reduce both to commodities, to be chosen or rejected like items in a supermarket, it concludes with some suggestions for moving beyond a culturally determined faith towards an encounter with the living God.

Chapter 1

Catholic Colleges and Universities in the United States

The network of Catholic colleges and universities in the United States today—some 235 institutions—is unique in the church. Most of these institutions were founded and administered by religious congregations to safeguard the faith and moral development of Catholic students in an often hostile Protestant culture.

In the mid-twentieth century, and especially after the Second Vatican Council (1962–65), these colleges and universities went through a process of growth and professionalization.[1] Enrollments increased, growing from 92,000 at the end of World War II to nearly 430,000 by 1970. New institutions were established. Standards were raised for students and faculty. New graduate programs were added, including an increasing number on the doctoral level. Faculty members were now expected to do research and publish. Core curricula were revised, dropping specifically confessional courses. Religion departments were transformed into more academic departments of theology or religious studies. Lay men and women were brought into positions of responsibility in university governance, while the 1967 Land O'Lakes statement, hammered out under the leadership of Notre Dame's Father Theodore Hesburgh, affirmed the principles of institutional autonomy and academic freedom.

Today most Catholic colleges and universities have entered the mainstream of American higher education; they are governed by boards of trustees comprised of both lay and religious members, the latter representatives of their sponsoring religious communities. Thus they are church related rather

---

1. See William P. Leahy, *Adapting to America: Catholics, Jesuits, and Higher Education in the Twentieth Century* (Washington, DC: Georgetown University Press, 1991) 123–54.

than canonically Catholic; like other institutions of higher learning, they value their institutional autonomy and their freedom of inquiry.

But as these institutions became more professional, their religious identities often suffered, the result of an identity crisis that has its roots in the 1960s. For many of them, a tendency to minimize Catholicism in their self-descriptions developed in order to attract a more diverse student body, gain financial support, or out of fear that the school be seen as "unwelcoming" or "oppressive" for others. The number of committed Catholic faculty and staff members continued to decline. Jesuit schools continued to stress their Jesuit character, though sometimes at the expense of their Catholic identity, partly in response to the marketing experts and branders who told them that "Jesuit sells, Catholic does not."[2] Often an "uneasy truce" prevailed. Too often the emphasis has been on what Catholics have in common with other churches and secular society rather than on what makes them unique.

At the end of his long study on Catholic higher education, *Contending with Modernity*, Philip Gleason comes to the following conclusion: "The task facing Catholic academics today is to forge from the philosophical and theological resources uncovered in the past half-century a vision that will provide what Neoscholasticism did for so many years—a theoretical rationale for the existence of Catholic colleges and universities as a distinctive element in American education."[3] In the last two decades, there has been a new emphasis on Catholic identity, with seminars on the Catholic tradition for new faculty, regional meetings of faculty and staff, and the appointment of vice presidents for mission and ministry—all efforts to address a diminished Catholic identity, especially with fewer clerical and religious representatives in the university community.

A related concern is the loss of faith for so many Catholics. According to a recent Pew Forum Study, one-third of those raised Catholic no longer identify with the church. Other Christian churches have experienced even greater losses.[4] Catholic colleges and universities, if they are to be authentically Catholic, need to be at the service of the faith, particularly for the next generation of Catholics. When Pope Benedict XVI visited the United States in April 2008, he said in an address to Catholic educators at the Catholic University of America that education "is integral to the mission of the Church. . . . First and foremost every Catholic educational institution is a

2. See David J. O'Brien, "Conversations on Jesuit (and Catholic?) Higher Education: Jesuit Sí, Catholic . . . No So Sure," in *A Jesuit Education Reader*, ed. George W. Traub (Chicago: Loyola Press, 2008) 217–31.

3. Philip Gleason, *Contending with Modernity: Catholic Higher Education in the Twentieth Century* (New York: Oxford University Press, 1995) 322.

4. See http://pewresearch.org/pubs/743/united-states-religion.

place to encounter the living God who in Jesus Christ reveals his transforming love and truth (cf. *Spe salvi* 4).[5]

In this chapter we will trace the development of Catholic higher education, from the network of colleges and universities that grew from the labors
of the newly founded Jesuit order in the sixteenth, seventeenth, and eighteenth centuries to the gradual transformation of Catholic colleges and universities in the United States in the twentieth century and especially after
the Second Vatican Council.

Jesuit Colleges

The Society of Jesus began as a movement of university students, gathered
around a charismatic former soldier from the Basque region of Spain, Ignatius
of Loyola (1491–1556). They had become friends at the University of Paris,
then the finest university in Europe. Originally a group of reformed priests,
their community was confirmed as a religious order by the bull of Pope Paul
III, *Regimini militantis ecclesiae*, on September 27, 1540. But the Jesuit
commitment to education which was later to distinguish the order was more
a providential development than something planned from the beginning.

The Jesuit ministerial commitment was threefold, spelled out in what is
called the *Formula of the Institute*, a document drawn up by the first companions which is to the Society of Jesus what most other religious orders
find in their Rule. According to the second version of the *Formula* (1550),
the Society was founded

> to strive especially for the defense and propagation of the faith and for the
> progress of souls in Christian life and doctrine, by means of public preach-
> ing, lectures, and any other ministrations whatsoever of the word of God,
> and further by means of the Spiritual Exercises, the education of children
> and unlettered person in Christianity, and the spiritual consolation of
> Christ's faithful through hearing confession and administering the other
> sacraments. Moreover, he should show himself ready to reconcile the
> estranged, compassionately assist and serve those who are in prisons and
> hospitals, and indeed to perform any other works of charity, according to
> what will seem expedient for the glory of God and the common good.[6]

Jesuits referred to these works as their "customary ministries" (*consueta
ministeria*). John O'Malley calls them the "ministries of the Word, of the

---

5. Benedict XVI, "Meeting with Catholic Educators," the Catholic University of America,
April 17, 2008.
6. See *The Constitutions of the Society of Jesus and Their Complementary Norms*, ed.
John W. Padberg (St. Louis: Institute of Jesuit Sources, 1996) no. 1.

sacraments, and of the works of mercy."[7] Note that schools are not mentioned, though the *Formula* does include "the education of children and unlettered persons in Christianity," what we would call today catechesis.

Though neither Ignatius nor any of his first companions took the doctorate in theology at Paris, a degree that required twelve to fourteen years, they "saw themselves and were seen by others" as theologians.[8] They had licentiates or the Master of Arts degree in philosophy and often addressed each other with the title "Master." After finishing their philosophy studies, all attended lectures in theology at the four colleges where theology was taught. Before long, the "ministries of the Word" saw some of them lecturing in theology at various universities, Diego Laínez and Pierre Favre at Rome in 1537, Favre at Mainz in 1542–43, and Claude Jay at Ingolstadt in 1543–44, though he declined the chair Johannes Eck had held there until his death in 1543. Ignatius, as the Father General, was granted permission to assign members of the Society to teach theology by the bull *Licet debitum* in 1549. Laínez and Alfonso Salmerón both served as official theologians for the Council of Trent, as did Jay, but briefly.

The Colleges

As early as 1541 these first Jesuits established a "college" at the University of Paris, but it was simply a residence for their young members who would study at the university and take classes at the other colleges. In 1542, lacking funding and with a war breaking out, the college at Paris was temporarily closed. The Jesuit students or "scholastics," as they were called, were sent to Louvain where another college was established. Other colleges followed, at Cologne, Padua, Alcalá, Valencia, and Coimbra, in addition to those at Paris and Louvain. But it was difficult to sustain these colleges without incomes, and few benefactors were interested in supporting institutions that served only the younger members of this new order. The exception was Coimbra in Portugal, opened in 1542 with the support of King John III and fully endowed by 1546.

As the young Society grew, a number of developments were to transform these colleges into schools in the more traditional sense. First, dismayed by the lack of education and formation for the diocesan priests in Germany where he was working, Jay proposed that the Society establish colleges for

---

7. John W. O'Malley, *The First Jesuits* (Cambridge, MA: Harvard University Press, 1993) 85.

8. Ibid., 243–45, at 243; the first companions included Francis Xavier, Diego Laínez, Pierre Favre, Alfonso Salmerón, Simâo Rodriques, Nicholás Bobadilla, Claude Jay, Paschase Broët, and Jean Codure.

training candidates for the priesthood, though he acknowledged that "our vocation is not ordered to undertaking professorships or 'ordinary' lecture-ships in the universities."[9] At about the same time, Ignatius had talked to Laínez about the possibility of introducing lectures into the colleges for the scholastics, in the manner of the colleges at Paris. In Spain, the Duke of Gandía, Francis Borgia, not yet a Jesuit, had helped establish a college. Eager for the education of the sons of his subjects who had converted from Islam, he petitioned Ignatius to have the Jesuits teach at the college, as there was no university in Gandía, and to admit non-Jesuit students. Ignatius agreed, and in 1542 the Jesuits there began teaching lay students. Pope Paul III designated the school a *studium generale*, that is, a university. As Michael Buckley notes, this "was not the last Jesuit instance of launching institutions bedecked with grand titles but sustained with slender resources."[10] In Asia, the Jesuits were already established in Goa where since 1543 some of them were instructing boys between the ages of ten and twenty in reading, writing, grammar, and catechism. By 1548 they had assumed responsibility for the institution. Finally, in 1547 the city fathers of Messina, Sicily, asked for Jesuits to staff a college which they promised to fund. Ignatius responded by sending ten Jesuits, six of them scholastics.

By now a new direction seemed to be emerging. With civic support the problem of support for the college had been solved, providing a model for future colleges. Jerome Nadal, who had been elected superior, apparently was enthusiastic about the effort; O'Malley says that "although relatively few of his letters from this period survive, they must have helped convince Ignatius and others to move with bold, even precipitous speed along a path where previously they had taken only a few tentative steps."[11]

Other colleges were quickly to follow: at Palermo in 1549, Naples and Venice in 1549, Rome in 1550, Cologne in 1557, and Macau (Asia) in 1585. The colleges thus became the principal centers for Jesuit ministries, particularly as Ignatius in his later years preferred to accept colleges with churches attached. At the time of his death in 1556, the Society was in charge of thirty-five or more colleges, many of them exclusively for lay students. Some were funded by princes or nobles, some by groups of interested citizens, some by individuals.

9. Cited in O'Malley, *The First Jesuits*, 203.
10. Michael J. Buckley, *The Catholic University as Promise and Project: Reflections in a Jesuit Idiom* (Washington, DC: Georgetown University Press, 1998) 58.
11. O'Malley, *The First Jesuits*, 204.

Jesuit Education

The program in Jesuit higher education from the beginning combined a humanistic education with professional or scholastic studies. The word *humanitas*, so important to the Renaissance humanists, came from Varro and Cicero who used it to translate the Greek *paideia*, which described the Greek ideal of educating a person into an adult capable of realizing the perfection of human nature so that he could take part in the life of the city-state or polis. The Renaissance *studia humanitatis* became *litterae human-iores* (Spanish *letras de humanidad*).[12] Influenced by the humanist movement, the early Jesuits were convinced that a humanistic education contributed to a virtuous life. Thus students in colleges followed a course of studies that stressed languages, "the arts or natural sciences" (logic, physics, metaphysics, moral philosophy, and mathematics), as well as religious formation and moral development. As O'Malley says, "the *pietas* of the humanists correlated with the inculcation of *Christianitas* that was their mission."[13]

As the educational efforts of the Jesuits developed, two different types of institutions emerged. First there were the colleges for students between the ages of ten and sixteen who followed a curriculum built around the "lower disciplines," referred to as "languages or humane letters"—grammar, poetry, history, rhetoric (which meant oratory), and languages, specifically Latin, Greek, and Hebrew. Given the age of the students, the colleges combined what in American schools would be both secondary and undergraduate education.

Then there were the universities. The medieval universities traditionally had four faculties: arts, theology, law, and medicine. In the *Constitutions* of the Society of Jesus, the term "university," appearing as *universitates vel studia generalia*, meant a college in which the lower faculty of languages and humane letters has been augmented by the higher faculties of language, the arts, and theology.[14] In the *modus parisiensis* that the Jesuits had adopted, based on their experience at Paris, the various disciplines constituted a pyramid: first the humane letters or "arts" (which O'Malley called the "undergraduate college"),[15] then philosophy (which included the natural sciences—logic, physics, metaphysics, and mathematics), with theology as its apex, though only those preparing for the priesthood took formal courses in theology. The Jesuit universities ordinarily did not include faculties of law or

12. See Buckley, *The Catholic University*, 93–95.

13. John W. O'Malley, "How the First Jesuits Became Involved in Education," in *A Jesuit Education Reader*, 51.

14. See George E. Ganss, *Saint Ignatius' Idea of a Jesuit University* (Milwaukee: Marquette University Press, 1954) 33; Constitutions, Part IV, nos. 498, 501; also Buckley, *The Catholic University*, 63.

15. O'Malley, "How the First Jesuits Became Involved in Education," 46.

medicine. Thus in this model of a university, which has remained the same in Europe down to the present day, theology is present in the university as a faculty or specialty; it is not integrated into the general curriculum. The Collegio Romano, later known simply as the Gregorian, was established in 1551 to train candidates for the priesthood. It was the first Jesuit university, and the Jesuits became the world's first teaching order.

Liam Brockey describes the typical program of studies for those Jesuit students who entered the Society at the universities of Coimbra or Évora in Portugal in the early seventeenth century and later went to China as missionaries. They began at the age of six or seven, progressing through Latin and some Greek grammar; then at the age of fourteen or fifteen they began their study of the humanities, Latin and Greek prose and poetry, the classical canon of Cicero, Virgil, Homer, Ovid, and Horace. Those who joined the Society did so at this point. They did the second and third academic cycles as scholastics— the arts course in Greek philosophy, Aristotle's works on natural philosophy and metaphysics, assisted by Jesuit commentaries, some mathematics, Euclid's *Elements*, and some astronomy. The third cycle was theology, two years of moral theology and casuistry, which included training in pastoral skills, and then two years of speculative theology (for those in the "long" course).[16]

The growing network of Jesuit colleges began to reshape the nature of education for both religious and lay students. Because the scholastics were expected to teach as well as study, they were generally sent to the larger colleges where they quickly became involved in a multitude of ministries. This and the fact that they studied alongside lay students made their own training quite different from that of the diocesan clergy, educated in the new system of seminaries mandated by the Council of Trent. It enriched the scholastics' training, but it also at times impeded their own studies.

The Modus Parisiensis

The *modus parisiensis* included a modular system which allowed students, divided into classes, to advance at their own rates from basic disciplines to more complicated ones. It also stressed active learning. Based on a combination of lectures and a variety of drills, repetitions, and disputations in which competition played a key role, the idea was to combine learning with skills appropriated through exercise (*exercitium*). The goal was often described as *eloquentia perfecta*, in both oral and written expression. Thus Jesuit schools became known for Latin disputations, oratory, and theater in all its aspects,

16. Liam Matthew Brockey, *Journey to the East: The Jesuit Mission to China, 1579–1724* (Cambridge, MA: Harvard University Press, 2007) 212–13.

including spectacles, music, dance, even ballet and drama, often conducted around biblical themes. For example, Jesuit scholastic José de Acosta, while still a fifteen-year-old student at Medina del Campo in Spain, wrote a drama in 1555 called *Jephthah Sacrificing His Daughter*. De Acosta would later distinguish himself for his work in Peru, studying Indian culture and languages and establishing guidelines for missionary work.[17] Dramatic productions or spectacles played an important role in the Jesuit colleges:

> The exuberance of school life continued to find a most colorful expression in drama. Variety in form and technical aspects continued to develop. Choruses and arias multiplied. Scenery became more elaborate, with calm lakes and restless seas, star filled heavens and lovely landscapes, building and battlements. Mechanical devices in the forms of explosives, lightning, and flying machines became more sophisticated. Highly trained orchestras accompanied the actors. In Munich in 1643 an orchestra of thirty-two pieces assisted at the performance of Theophilus.[18]

But Jesuit education stressed more than the arts. The collegiate churches attached to their colleges helped support the work of architects, painters, and sculptors, while the astronomical observatories and laboratories in their larger schools and the letters and natural objects sent back for display by Jesuit missionaries laboring far from Europe contributed to the cultivation of the sciences.[19] Jesuit professors included scholars like Christopher Clavius (1538–1612), a mathematician and astronomer responsible for the Gregorian calendar, and Athanasius Kircher (1601–80), a polymath credited as the founder of Egyptology. O'Malley attributes the openness to culture of Jesuit missionaries like Matteo Ricci in China and Roberto de Nobili in India to the humanist education that the Society provided for its own members.[20]

Originally tuition free, the Jesuit schools accepted students from all classes, though some sought to serve the poor. But because their education was more humanistic than practical, focused on basic skills, the Jesuits tended to attract students from the upper classes. Protestant students were admitted, though they were often excused from specifically Catholic religious practices, and "heretical" books were confiscated.

17. Claudio M. Burgaleta, *José de Acosta, S.J. (1540–1600)* (Chicago: Loyola Press, 1999) 14.

18. William V. Bangert, *A History of the Society of Jesus* (St. Louis: The Institute of Jesuit Sources, 1986) 131–32; see Brockey's description of the elaborate spectacle at Évora, celebrating the occasion of the canonization of Ignatius and Xavier in 1622, in *Journey to the East*, 207.

19. See O'Malley, "How the Jesuits Became Involved in Education," 58–59; also John W. O'Malley, ed. *The Jesuits: Cultures, Sciences, and the Arts, 1540–1733* (Toronto: University of Toronto Press, 1999).

20. O'Malley, "How the First Jesuits Became Involved in Education," 56.

Spiritual Formation

Only those preparing for the priesthood studied theology, as we have already mentioned. But the education in the colleges was not restricted to the humanities. The Jesuits hoped to communicate to their students a "learned piety" (*docta pietas*), to make them "good citizens." As O'Malley says, "[u]nder the influence of Quintilian and other theorists, the Jesuits looked more to formation of mind and character, to *Bildung*, than to the acquisition of ever more information or the advancement of the disciplines."[21] Thus they added to their curriculum a weekly class in Christian doctrine as well as "cases of conscience," though it is not always clear how they functioned; presumably they were to teach students how to make moral decisions. Each college also included a spiritual program, usually consisting of frequent or daily attendance at Mass, participation in the liturgical hours, the examination of conscience, confession, fasts and other penances, and Holy Communion at determined intervals. Students were expected to practice charitable service to others, known as the works of mercy. Later they were encouraged to make the Spiritual Exercises.

Thus from the beginning the Jesuits offered the same kind of personal attention to the gifts and needs of their students that their *Constitutions* prescribed their religious superiors to exercise in regard to the Jesuits themselves. Today that care for the individual student is referred to in Jesuit language as *cura personalis*.

The Marian Congregations

Characteristic of the Jesuit efforts to form their students religiously were the Marian congregations. They represented a Jesuit adaptation of the confraternities that played a major role in the development of the church's devotional life in the late Middle Ages. Often sponsored by the Dominican or Franciscan orders and sharing in their spiritualities, the confraternities offered lay men and women a way to live a more intense devotional life, to take a more active part in the church's ministry to the world and particularly to the poor.[22] It is thought that the first Jesuit confraternity was founded by Pierre Favre at Parma in 1539–40.

The first Marian congregation for students was established by a young Belgian Jesuit, Father Jean Leunis, at the Roman College in 1563. Leunis

21. O'Malley, *The First Jesuits*, 214.
22. See Christopher F. Black, *Italian Confraternities in the Sixteenth Century* (Cambridge, England: Cambridge University Press, 1989); Maureen Flynn, *Sacred Charity: Confraternities and Social Welfare in Spain, 1400–1700* (Ithaca, NY: Cornell University Press, 1989).

gathered a group of boys in their early teens who dedicated themselves to various exercises of piety, among them daily Mass, weekly confession, monthly Communion, a half-hour meditation each day, and a commitment to "serve the poor." Leunis' congregation in Rome was to set the pattern for the Jesuit colleges. The students were committed to a program of regular prayer, the sacraments of penance and the Eucharist, and to works of charity. Leunis later established Marian congregations at Paris, Billom, Lyons, and Avignon, and they spread to the other Jesuit colleges. By 1575 all the colleges at the University of Paris had Marian congregations, one of which chose Francis de Sales, then a student, as prefect. Edmund Campion founded one in the college at Prague in 1575, while Peter Canisius established one at the University of Ingolstadt in 1577 and another at Fribourg in 1582. Though not all the Marian congregations were college based, by 1576 there were 30,000 students in Marian congregations at the Jesuit colleges of Europe.[23] In 1584 Pope Gregory XIII issued *Omnipotentis Dei*, a bull recognizing the Marian congregation in Rome as the *Prima primaria*, the primary congregation to which other congregations were to be "aggregated."

A Marian congregation, or Sodality of Our Lady as it would be known in English-speaking countries, would be directed by "one of the fathers" and have a "prefect" elected from one of "the older and wiser" boys.[24] Francis Coster, provincial of Germany, supplied a guidebook for the Marian congregations in his *Libellus sodalitatis*, which became the basis for a succession of handbooks down to the twentieth century. It included a consecration to the Blessed Virgin that gradually became universal. If some congregations adopted the tradition of penitential processions, especially during Holy Week, they also channeled the energies of the students of the colleges into spectacular celebrations of feast days:

> Those of the Sodality of the College of La Flèche were renowned: hymns, vespers, processions, high pontifical Masses, meetings and literary expositions, theatrical plays, pastorals, illuminations . . . succeeded each other for several days. In one of these processions 1,250 externs were counted, 250 boarders, 200 Sodalists with penants [sic], banners, standards, followed by ecclesiastics and religious of different Orders, civic authorities to make it complete, and preceded by a band to stir up 20 parishes.[25]

23. Bangert, *A History of the Society of Jesus*, 57.
24. O'Malley, *The First Jesuits*, 198.
25. Louis Paulussen, *Abridged History of the Sodalities of Our Lady* (St. Louis, MO: The Queen's Work, 1957) 49; from Emile Villaret, *Congrégations mariales* (Paris: Beau Chesne, 1947).

In 1967 the World Federation of Marian Congregations changed its name to World Federation of Christian Life Communities.

The School Masters of Europe

This Jesuit commitment to education marked a new departure in the history of the Catholic Church; no other religious order had undertaken such a ministry, and they went about it systematically. Ignatius devoted the last part of his *Constitutions* to the colleges and universities, drafting its chapters two years before he died. While most of the *Constitutions* came from his own hand, he drew on the assistance of Diego Laínez, Juan de Polanco, and André des Freux in developing chapters 11 to 17 of Part IV, dealing with the universities of the Society. These three fathers represented the wide experience the early Jesuits had with university education, having studied at Paris, Alcalá, and Padua respectively.

Some fifty years of academic experience and educational planning bore fruit in 1599 with the publication of the *Ratio studiorum*, a plan for the organization of studies within the Society. It was not so much a philosophy of education as a set of rules or a "codification of curricular, administrative, and pedagogical principles"[26] for all those involved in Jesuit schools—rectors, professors of the different disciplines, students, both Jesuit scholastics and non-Jesuit students, and "beadles" or teacher's assistants—with a careful attention to goals.[27] While remarkably specific about teaching methods, competitions, examinations, spiritual practices, subject matter for essays, and discipline, at the same time it needs to be understood against the background of the *Constitutions*, particularly Part IV. Ignatius counseled a conformity in regard to the academic program in a given region, but he also stressed that it be adapted according to the needs of places, times, and persons.[28] One commentator suggested that the *Ratio*'s greatest contribution to our times was the idea of the curriculum as the primary vehicle for the mission of the university.[29]

While the Jesuits were indebted to other groups or movements, including the Brethren of the Common Life, Scholasticism, Renaissance humanism, and the *modus parisiensis*, the *Ratio* is unique. So was the network of schools the Society established. Tuition free, they were endowed or funded by local

---

26. O'Malley, "How the Jesuits Became Involved in Education," 57.

27. *The Ratio Studiorum: The Official Plan for Jesuit Education*, translation and commentary by Claude N. Pavur (St. Louis: Institute of Jesuit Sources, 2005).

28. Constitutions, no. 455.

29. Claude N. Pavur, "The Curriculum Carries the Mission," *Conversations* 34 (Fall 2008) 30.

communities, able to accept students on merit rather than social status. By 1625 they had 372 colleges. At the time of the suppression of the Society in 1773, Jesuits were involved in some 800 educational institutions from Europe to Asia and Latin America, including 15 of their own universities.

When the Society was restored in 1814, the Jesuits' buildings and income-producing properties had been confiscated. The secularization which followed the French Revolution meant that higher education remained for the most part in government hands. The old Jesuit network was not reestablished. Even today, wandering through historic cities in Europe one finds buildings that once housed Jesuit colleges or streets that bear names like *Jesuitengasse* or *Calle de la Compañía*. Little wonder that the Jesuits earned the sobriquet "schoolmasters of Europe." Among famous graduates of Jesuit schools can be numbered Descartes, Peter Paul Rubens, Molière, Voltaire, Francis de Sales, and Charles Carroll, and in more recent times Tip O'Neill, Fidel Castro, Bill Clinton, and Tim Russert. More than 9 percent of the 111th U.S. Congress are graduates of Jesuit colleges and universities.

After the restoration of the Society, Jesuit efforts were confined for the most part to secondary education, though Jesuit universities were to flourish again in America.[30] But they were no longer tuition free. With encouragement from Rome, the Jesuit General allowed Jesuit colleges to begin charging fees in 1833.[31] Today there are some ninety Jesuit colleges in twenty-seven countries throughout the world.

Catholic Higher Education in the United States

In the United States most Catholic colleges and universities are sponsored by religious orders. While the Jesuit network is the largest, with twenty-eight institutions and over a million living graduates, it is not the only one.[32] The various Franciscan congregations sponsor twenty colleges and universities; the Sisters of Mercy, nineteen; the Dominicans, eighteen; and the Brothers of the Christian Schools (Christian Brothers), seven. These Catholic institutions of higher education were to undergo a threefold transformation in the early decades of the twentieth century.

---

30. Ganss, *St. Ignatius' Idea of a Jesuit University*, 4.

31. See Gilbert J. Garraghan, *The Jesuits in the Middle United States*, vol. 1 (New York: America Press, 1938) 304–08.

32. At the beginning of the 111th Congress (2009), Catholics constituted the largest religious group in the Congress, 29 percent, with 9 percent Jesuit educated.

From a European to an American Model

The first transformation was from a predominantly European college system to an American model. As the century opened, there were approximately five dozen Catholic colleges in the United States sponsored by religious orders, almost half of them administered by the Jesuits.[33] Most were still constructed on a European model, whether based on the French *lycée*, the German gymnasium, or the old Jesuit liberal arts college, which combined secondary and baccalaureate studies in one seven-year program. As Philip Gleason says in his study of Catholic higher education in the twentieth century:

> whereas non-Catholic educators thought of secondary and collegiate work as belonging to two different levels, with the college being properly confined to strictly post-secondary work, Catholics were heirs to the Continental tradition in which the college functioned as a combined secondary-collegiate institution whose course of studies lasted for six years or so and was followed (for the few who continued their education) by specialized professional studies at the university level.[34]

While the differences between preparatory and properly collegiate work were not always that distinct in both the Catholic and non-Catholic institutions, the latter began to professionalize in the last three decades of the nineteenth century. As they began to expand their subject areas, introduce elective courses, majors, departments, and professional schools, and develop accrediting programs and admission standards, these colleges were transformed into modern universities.

The hostility from an academic culture still predominantly Protestant and moving in the direction of "nonsectarian" institutions also contributed to the modernization of Catholic higher education. For example, in 1898 Harvard University established a policy excluding graduates of Jesuit colleges from the list of those who would be admitted to Harvard's Law School, though an exception was made for Georgetown University, which was at least initially included on the list, "lest it should seem to some persons that the Catholic colleges had been excluded on religious grounds."[35]

---

33. Kathleen A. Mahoney, *Catholic Higher Education in Protestant America: The Jesuits and Harvard in the Age of the University* (Baltimore and London: Johns Hopkins University Press, 2003) 6.

34. See Gleason, *Contending with Modernity*, 4; see also his "Catholic Higher Education as Historical Context for Theological Education," in *Theological Education in the Catholic Tradition*, ed. Patrick W. Carey and Earl C. Muller (New York: Crossroad, 1997) 24–25; I am grateful to Gleason for this overview.

35. Mahoney, quoting Harvard's president Charles W. Eliot, in *Catholic Higher Education in Protestant America*, 79. Eliot's objections were based particularly on his belief that Jesuit

Thus Catholic institutions at the beginning of the twentieth century were forced to change.[36] They began to standardize the kind of education secondary schools were expected to provide and to redefine their colleges as postsecondary institutions, with clear entrance requirements, multiple departments, and 120 units required for graduation.[37] Catholic educators began to take a more active role in non-Catholic educational associations. With thousands of World War II veterans entering college, thanks to the GI Bill, enrollment at Catholic colleges and universities mushroomed.

The Jesuits also adapted, but slowly. According to Mahoney, their adaptation "through the mid-twentieth century did not entail a complete concession to modernity, but rather a mix of adaptation and resistance that ensured Jesuit higher education of a distinctive Catholic identity until well into the twentieth century."[38] The Jesuit Educational Association, established in 1934, tried to coordinate Jesuit educational programs against the provincialism endemic to the Society, and increasingly stressed graduate education.

Philosophy and Catholic Identity

A second transformation resulted from new concerns about Catholic identity. As Catholic schools began to look more like other colleges and universities, both in academic programs and in student life, educators began to ask what made them specifically Catholic. The answer was provided by privileging Neo-Scholastic philosophy in the curriculum. Philosophy of course was not new to Catholic higher education; it had long been part of the traditional liberal arts program, along with classical languages, but in the 1920s philosophy began to assume the dominant role in the core curriculum, reinforced by the church's campaign against modernism. Indeed it could be seen as the integrating discipline, since philosophy meant Neoscholastic philosophy studied systematically, providing an intellectual framework or "worldview" for Catholic thought.[39] The founding of the American Catholic Philosophical Association (1926) and journals such as *The Modern Schoolman* (1925) and *The New Scholasticism* (1927) contributed to this, as did the "Catholic Renaissance" represented by rising stars Jacques Maritain and Étienne Gilson.

---

education had not changed since the sixteenth century and that Jesuit students were denied the opportunity to elect their own courses, 82–86.

36. See Leahy, "American Catholicism vs. Academic Professionalism," in *Adapting to America*, 33–65.

37. Gleason, "Catholic Higher Education," 25.

38. Mahoney, *Catholic Higher Education in Protestant America*, 242.

39. Melanie M. Morey and John J. Piderit, *Catholic Higher Education: A Culture in Crisis* (Oxford: Oxford University Press, 2006) 129.

Thus at most Catholic colleges and universities students took an equivalent minor in scholastic philosophy. At Jesuit institutions they went through a systematic program of logic, philosophy of nature, philosophy of man, epistemology, natural theology, general ethics, and applied ethics, taking a philosophy course every semester. At Boston College in the 1950s a student took an exceptional ten courses in philosophy, twenty-eight units, during his last two years.[40] But all that began to change in the 1960s. Boston College reduced its requirements in philosophy to five courses, fifteen units, in 1963–64. In 1962 Georgetown required twenty-five hours of philosophy, but that was reduced to eighteen units in 1963, twelve by 1967, and six by 1970.[41] At Gonzaga University in the late 60s seniors had to sit for oral examinations in philosophy, administered by faculty and some of the Jesuit scholastics who were themselves finishing degrees in philosophy.

But, Gleason asks, why philosophy rather than theology?[42] The answer is simple. Prior to the Second Vatican Council, the study of theology took place largely in seminaries; it was a clerical endeavor, taught by priests for seminarians. The Catholic University of America represented a significant exception, thanks to the work of John Montgomery Cooper (1881–1949), a priest of the diocese of Washington; it began exploring the idea of undergraduate theology as early as 1909. In 1920 Cooper founded a department of religion for undergraduates. He did not call it a department of theology, in order to differentiate the discipline he was developing from what was done in seminaries. His intention was to integrate the church's devotional and liturgical life with its doctrinal teaching, unlike the formalistic, compartmentalized, Latin manuals used in the seminaries. However, his Augustinian approach to theology meant that undergraduate theological education was primarily moral, rather than intellectual; it was designed to lead students to love of God and neighbors.[43]

Cooper's program was the exception. For the most part, students in Catholic colleges and universities, including Jesuit ones, did not study theology; they took supplemental courses in "religion." The courses were largely apologetic in nature, concerned with doctrinal orthodoxy and religious formation. They met fewer hours per week, received less academic credit,

---

40. James Tunstead Burtchaell, *The Dying of the Light: The Disengagement of Colleges and Universities from their Christian Roots* (Grand Rapids, MI: William B. Eerdmans, 1998) 577.

41. Ibid., 578 and 720, n. 35.

42. Gleason, "Catholic Higher Education," 26.

43. See Patrick W. Carey, "College Theology in Historical Perspective," in *American Catholic Traditions: Resources for Renewal*, ed. Sandra Yocum Mize and William Portier (Maryknoll, NY: Orbis Books, 1997) 248–49.

and were taught by priest instructors who lacked the academic credentials increasingly expected in other departments. At my own university, religion courses met two hours per week for one unit of credit (rather than the usual three). This was true of most Catholic colleges.[44] As late as 1937, only three Catholic colleges out of a sample of eighty-four offered an academic major in religion.[45]

Yet as early as the second decade of the twentieth century, some educators and theologians were raising questions about the inferior character of religious education in Catholic colleges, including Jesuit ones. William P. Leahy points out that in "the 1920s and early 1930s, certain Jesuits and influential alumni . . . judged that philosophy and religion classes were academically weak and poorly taught" in Jesuit colleges.[46] In 1939, the National Catholic Alumni Federation sponsored a symposium calling for a "return" of theology to the college curriculum.[47] One of the participants in the symposium, Jesuit theologian John Courtney Murray, agreed; but he argued that the kind of theology taught in seminaries would have to be rethought.[48] In a famous article, published later in *Theological Studies*, he maintained that the colleges should begin developing theology courses "for the layman."[49] He was joined by other Jesuits, arguing that "religion or theology" should have "primacy of place" and should be the integrating discipline in the curriculum.[50] Throughout the 1940s and 1950s one finds repeated complaints in the *Jesuit Educational Quarterly* about the secondary status of "religion" courses in Jesuit colleges; one Jesuit complained that religion courses received, not the usual three semester credit hours, but only one, "the same amount they get for public speaking."[51] But change was in the works.

44. See Robert J. Wister, "The Teaching of Theology 1950–1990: The American Catholic Experience," *America* 162 (February 3, 1990) 92.

45. Gleason, "Catholic Higher Education," 26–27.

46. Leahy, *Adapting to America*, 36.

47. Gleason, *Contending with Modernity*, 164; Gleason notes that the term "return" was used "mistakenly."

48. Ibid., 165.

49. John Courtney Murray, "Towards a Theology for the Layman: The Problem of Its Finality," *Theological Studies* 5 (1944) 43–75; also "Towards a Theology for the Layman: The Pedagogical Problem," *Theological Studies* 5 (1944) 340–76.

50. William A. Huesman, "Integration of College Studies by Means of Theology," *Jesuit Educational Quarterly* 15 (1952) 30; Gerald van Ackeren made the same point in his "Reflections on the Relation between Philosophy and Theology," *Theological Studies* 14 (1953) 548.

51. Eugene B. Gallagher, "A College Religion Course: Problems," *Jesuit Educational Quarterly* 12 (1949) 95.

From Philosophy to Theology

In the 1950s several scholars began raising questions about the undistinguished character of Catholic higher education. In 1955 John Tracy Ellis, a professor of church history at the Catholic University of America, published "American Catholics and the Intellectual Life," arguing that Catholic schools were concerned much more with moral development than with intellectual excellence, and thus contributed little to the intellectual life of the country.[52] Thomas O'Dea took his argument further, identifying certain negatives within the Catholic tradition itself, among them a formalism, clericalism, authoritarianism, and defensiveness that worked against genuine intellectual accomplishment.[53] Others saw the dominant Neoscholastic philosophy as part of an outmoded Catholic rationalism, closed to newer developments in philosophy such as phenomenology, existentialism, and language analysis. But the uproar that followed in 1963 when Monsignor William J. McDonald, the rector of the Catholic University of America, struck the names of Jesuits John Courtney Murray and Gustave Weigel, liturgical scholar Godfrey Diekmann, O.S.B., and the young Swiss theologian Hans Küng from a list of speakers prepared by the Graduate Student Council evidenced the change that was underway.

In the period after the Second Vatican Council, both Catholic undergraduate curricula and the discipline of theology itself changed considerably. As colleges and universities began to rethink their curricula, the emphasis on philosophy was reduced considerably, from virtually every semester to four courses, and then often just two. Religion departments upgraded and professionalized, introducing courses in theology or religious studies and changing their names to reflect these changes in the discipline. By 1985 the twenty-eight Jesuit colleges and universities required an average of eight semester hours of philosophy and 7.5 credits in theology,[54] an average that has changed little since then. As philosophy departments became increasingly pluralistic, theology was placed in the position of being the standard-bearer for the institution's Catholic identity (a role it did not always accept), and new departments of campus ministry took the place formerly held by the university chaplain.

---

52. John Tracy Ellis, "American Catholics and the Intellectual Life," *Thought* 30/118 (1955) 351–88.

53. Thomas O'Dea, *American Catholic Dilemma: An Inquiry into the Intellectual Life* (New York: Sheed and Ward, 1958).

54. Leahy, *Adapting to America*, 156.

Conclusion

In the twentieth century the long process of adapting Catholic colleges and universities to the different academic culture of the United States changed them from European style liberal arts colleges to American institutions of higher education, as we have seen. From originally being institutions dominated by clergy and members of religious orders, they have become increasingly lay in their faculty and administration. If none are ranked among America's elite institutions,[55]some have become highly respected, with doctoral programs and international reputations. The percentage of lay teachers increased from perhaps 10 to 15 percent in 1900 to 85 to 90 percent in 1980. At the same time, the number of non-Catholics teaching theology increased: to 50 percent at Seattle University in the late 1970s, 42 percent of full-time faculty at Marquette in 1977, and almost 40 percent at Notre Dame in 1984, reflecting the growing pluralism of church-related schools.[56]

But many perceptive commentators worry about whether Catholic institutions are really Catholic today. Are they still committed to the search for truth, which is really the search for God? Can they still be described as the place where the church does its thinking, as Notre Dame's Theodore Hesburgh liked to say? Do they truly form their students in the faith that does justice, or do they simply speed their passage into successful corporate lifestyles? Do they justify the high tuition that many Catholic parents can no longer afford? And are they significantly different from less expensive state institutions, or from other private colleges and universities?

Catholicism is supposed to be present in the theology and philosophy departments, but an appreciation for the Catholic tradition is often virtually absent from other departments. It should permeate all areas of the universities, not remain unknown. A 2009 graduate of Loyola University of Chicago wrote, "I asked several faculty members for their opinions on the integration of Catholic thought on a diverse campus, and most could not answer the questions frankly and instead referred me to speak to others on campus."[57] What Hesburgh wrote about Notre Dame should be true of every Catholic university: it "should reflect profoundly, and with unashamed commitment, its belief in the existence of God and in God's total revelation to us, especially through the Christian message; the deep, age-long mystery of salvation in history; and the inner, inalienable dignity and rights of every individual human person."[58]

55. Ibid., 135.
56. Ibid., 100–02.
57. Jennifer Sikora, "Faith and Religion Are Choices," *Conversations* 36 (Fall 2009) 48.
58. Hesburgh, *The Challenge and Promise of a Catholic University*, 8.

But Hesburgh is speaking to the ideal. As Paul Crowley notes, Jesuit universities in the United States have adopted the U.S. model of the corporate university and the values and standards of secular academic culture. "While there have been sound reasons for taking this direction, even the most ardent supporters of the current shape of Jesuit higher education would not claim that this has been done without cost, and in some cases, compromise to the essential Ignatian vision, especially as reformulated by recent Congregations."[59] This is true not only of Jesuit institutions. The emphasis in recent years on hiring for mission, Catholic Studies, learning communities, and vice presidents for mission and ministry are symbolic of a new concern for Catholic identity.

Even if contemporary Catholic colleges and universities are church related rather than canonically Catholic, they remain Catholic institutions. But how this works out in practice is not always clear, as was evident in the spring of 2009 when the University of Notre Dame invited the United States' newly elected and first African American president, Barack Obama to deliver the commencement address and receive an honorary degree. Some eighty bishops from across the United States protested, questioning Notre Dame's Catholicity because of Obama's virtually unqualified support for the "right" to abortion. Many of these bishops argue that abortion is so serious a moral issue that it surpasses all others. Others argue that, serious as it is, abortion must be seen against the full spectrum of Catholic social doctrine, including its teaching on war, human rights, and global poverty, and that "single issue" politics, given the nature of American politics, risks making the church seem to endorse a single political party, even to the extent of excommunicating candidates who support pro-choice positions, and thus is sectarian.[60]

An institution's Catholic identity has particular implications for theology as well: "theological research undertaken within a Catholic university is in the interest of not simply pure knowledge, but of knowledge at the service of faith, which includes, in the teachings of the Roman magisterium, the promotion of justice. Loss of this essential ecclesial dimension of the Catholic university is the loss of the soul of theology."[61]

In the next chapter we will consider more carefully the history of theology in the university and what faith and theology mean for Catholic colleges and universities today.

59. Paul G. Crowley, "Theology in the Jesuit University," in *The Jesuit Tradition in Education and Mission: A 450-Year Perspective*," ed. Christopher Chapple (Scranton: University of Scranton Press, 1993) 157.

60. For two views see "A Pastoral Reflection on the Controversy at Notre Dame," *America* 201/5 (2009); John M Darcy, "The Church and the University," 13–16; and John R. Quinn, "The Public Duty of Bishops," 18–21.

61. Crowley, "Theology in the Jesuit University," 161.

Chapter 2

Theology and the University

Theology has been at home in the university since the end of the twelfth century, when students and scholars began to organize themselves into collective bodies or "universities" in towns such as Bologna, Paris, and Oxford. As the universities began to take the place of the monastic or cathedral schools, they generally included a faculty of theology. By 1250, the University of Paris had four faculties: arts, law, medicine, and theology. Distinguished professors of the theology faculty at Paris included Alexander of Hales, Albert the Great, Thomas Aquinas, Bonaventure, Jean Gerson, Siger of Brabant, and Meister Eckhart, who was an alumnus.

Theology also held pride of place in the universities of the Society of Jesus. In its _Constitutions_ Ignatius wrote: "Since the end of the Society and of its studies is to aid our fellowmen to the knowledge and love of God and to the salvation of their souls, and since the subject of theology is the means most suited to this end, in the universities of the Society the principal emphasis ought to be placed upon it."[1] After their preparation in the humanities, those doing theology in Jesuit universities studied Sacred Scripture, scholastic theology, and positive theology, a discipline directed towards practice which examined the doctrines of the faith in light of their sources in Scripture, tradition, and canon law.[2] This progression was based on the _modus parisiensis_ that the first Jesuits had learned in their theological studies at Paris, though as Lawrence Cunningham points out, the idea that the liberal arts constituted the necessary prerequisite for theology goes back as far as Augustine, who argued in his _De doctrina Christiana_ for the study of pagan rhetorical learning as a preparation for the study of Scripture. The Jesuits

1. The _Constitutions of the Society of Jesus and Their Complementary Norms,_ ed. John W. Padberg (St. Louis: Institute of Jesuit Sources, 1996) no. 466.
2. _Constitutions,_ no. 446, note 1; see also Paul G. Crowley, "Theology in the Jesuit University," in _The Jesuit Tradition in Education and Mission: A 450-Year Perspective,_ ed. Christopher Chapple (Scranton: University of Scranton Press, 1993) 159.

institutionalized this progression from the arts to philosophy, and finally theology in their *Constitutions* (1556).[3]

The standard textbook for medieval theology was Peter Lombard's *Liber sententiarum*, but in the sixteenth century Dominican scholars were shifting to the *Summa theologiae* of Thomas Aquinas. Ignatius also adopted Aquinas as the primary text for Jesuit universities. But Jesuit theology should not be seen as a narrow scholasticism. It is rooted, as Michael Buckley argues, in Ignatius' vision of the relationship between the divine and the human; Jesuit education "comes out of a spirituality, out of a pattern or manner of living under the experience and empowerment of grace, that Ignatius presented as a way to God."[4] This spirituality has its roots in the Spiritual Exercises, particularly in the vision of the Contemplation for Obtaining Love (nos. 230–37), which envisions God's active presence in all creation, pouring out gifts, dwelling in creatures, working in them, with all good things descending from above.

Thus theology in a Jesuit university was never seen as simply one of the sciences; it held pride of place because Ignatius saw it as essentially pastoral, ordered to the Society's goal of bringing others to the knowledge and love of God. At the same time, for Ignatius, theology belonged in a university in its own right. As Buckley interprets Ignatius' vision, theology functioned as an architectonic wisdom, one that integrated and brought into order the different sciences, disciplines, subject matters, and activities of the university as it explored God's revelation.[5]

To continue our consideration of theology in the university, we will consider the ecclesial role played by theologians in the Middle Ages, the gradual transformation of theology from a sapiential or pastoral discipline to a critical one, the declericalization and laicization of theology in the twentieth century, and the present state of theology in Catholic colleges and universities in the United States.

The Magisterium of the Doctors

Theologians have always seen themselves as being at the service of the church. In the Middle Ages, the university theologians or *doctores* (who of course were clerics) collaborated with the hierarchy by serving on

3. Lawrence S. Cunningham, "The Undergraduate Theology Major," in *Theological Education in the Catholic Tradition*, ed. Patrick W. Carey and Earl C. Muller (New York: Crossroad, 1997) 98–99.

4. Michael J. Buckley, *The Catholic University as Promise and Project: Reflections in a Jesuit Idiom* (Washington, DC: Georgetown University Press, 1998) 81.

5. Buckley, *The Catholic University*, 71–72.

commissions which evaluated theological positions; they condemned those considered heterodox and even prepared papal censures. Avery Dulles pointed out that the "doctrinal decrees of several general councils (Lyons I, 1245; Lyons II, 1274; and Vienne, 1312) were submitted to universities for approval before being published."[6] From the thirteenth to the sixteenth centuries the masters of theology at the University of Paris issued censures on junior faculty members for doctrinal errors or were asked to lend their authority, based on their expertise, to authoritative judgments of bishops or popes.[7] Thomas Aquinas spoke of two *magisteria* or teaching offices. The bishops, with their supervisory responsibility, held the "magisterium of the pastoral chair" (*magisterium cathedrae pastoralis*); the theologians or doctors, whose competence was based on learning and scholarship, held the "magisterium of the professor's chair" (*magisterium cathedrae magistralis*).[8] Thus the important role theologians played in the life of the church was clearly recognized.

But because theology has also played a critical role vis-à-vis the tradition itself, distinguishing the church's official teaching from popular belief and theological opinion and reinterpreting its language so that it might better reflect the faith it is intended to express, there has often been tension between theologians and the church. The work of Aquinas did not go without question during his lifetime. Several of his teachings were included in a broader list of 219 propositions condemned by his bishop, the Bishop of Paris, as well as by the Archbishop of Canterbury three years after his death. As happened not infrequently, Aquinas was later declared a doctor of the church,

The authority of the masters or doctors of theology continued to grow until it began to conflict with that of the bishops. They voted at the councils of Constance (1414–18), Basel (1431–49), and Florence (1438–45), sometimes outvoting the bishops.[9] Since Florence, the church has understood a council as exercising the authority of the universal church when the assembled bishops act with and under the pope. But even after Florence, theologians continued to play an active role in councils. At Trent, they served on some of the congregations and spoke at the plenary sessions, including some from the Society of Jesus. But as the medieval synthesis gave way to modernity, the nature of theology was to change.

6. Avery Dulles, *A Church to Believe In* (New York: Crossroad, 1982) 109.

7. J. M. M. H. Thijssen, *Censure and Heresy at the University of Paris 1200–1400* (Philadelphia: University of Pennsylvania Press, 1998) 113–16.

8. Yves Congar, "A Semantic History of the Term 'Magisterium,'" in *Readings in Moral Theology, No. 3, The Magisterium and the Theologian*, ed. Charles E. Curran and Richard A. McCormick (New York: Paulist Press, 1982) 303; (Cf. Quodl. III 9 ad 3).

9. See Nelson H. Minnich, "The Voice of Theologians in General Councils from Pisa to Trent," *Theological Studies* 59/3 (1998) 426–29.

From Christian Wisdom to Critical Discipline

Theology as taught in the monastic schools represented a Christian wisdom. The basic theological form was the commentary, with monastic teachers commenting on the texts of Scripture, reading them in faith, appealing to various *auctores* in the tradition, especially the fathers of the church. But in the twelfth century, as the locus for theology changed from the monastery to the university, theology began to move in a new direction. The schoolmen or masters (*magistri* or *scholastici*) began to address the texts more critically, using the *quaestio* to investigate their objective substance, anticipating the *quaestio disputata* or disputed questions of the thirteen century, and producing systematic summaries of doctrine or *summae*.[10]

By the thirteenth century the rediscovery of Aristotle's thought was challenging the hegemony of the largely Platonic-Augustinian theology dominant in the West. As philosophy began to move in the direction of an autonomous discipline based on reason, a split began to develop between the Franciscan tradition and the Dominican. This can best be seen in the different approaches of two contemporaries, Bonaventure and Aquinas, to the relationship of faith and reason. For Bonaventure, the great Franciscan doctor of the church, theology was a wisdom grounded in Christ; he saw Scripture as the key to all truth, including that of the sciences. Thus philosophy had to be radically Christian. Aquinas took a different approach. He emphasized the difference between knowledge based on reason and that which comes only through faith. Thus he distinguished between the proper objects of the different sciences while allowing them their own proper roles in the theological task. Theology was a science that integrated sacred doctrine with philosophical reflection. Furthermore, his thought was enriched by contact with Jewish and Muslim sources.

But as reason probed the limits of faith, theology began to discern its own limits and became more critical. In the period after the Renaissance, theology was increasingly seen as one science alongside others; it was no longer an integrating or "architectonic" wisdom, illuminating the work of other sciences, deepening their insights in light of the wisdom of God taught by Sacred Scripture.[11]

Theology in Modernity

Though the Reformers sought to found theology anew on Scripture, post-Enlightenment Protestant theology underwent a profound change. Biblical

10. See Marie-Dominique Chenu, *Nature, Man, and Society in the Twelfth Century* (Chicago: University of Chicago Press, 1968) 291–309.
11. See Buckley, *The Catholic University*, 174–77.

theology, which had been a normative discipline, was transformed into a critical one.[12] Religion was to be investigated "objectively." As Sandra Schneiders points out: having rejected the authority of the Roman Church, the Reformers ultimately ended up adopting the Enlightenment principle that free critical investigation, not authority, is the ultimate criterion of truth. For biblical studies, this meant that the Bible was to be investigated by the same methods as any other historical text. But this implied that the Bible for all practical purposes was itself just a historical text, rather than a theological reality, a revelatory text.[13]

Catholicism was slower to develop a critical theology. Put on the defensive by the Reformation, Catholic theology became increasingly apologetic and deductive. Authority, centered in Rome, became a primary theological source, exercised by an authoritarian church office to protect the faithful from heterodox works. The old inquisition was transformed into a Roman congregation by Pope Paul III in 1542. Pope Paul IV created the Index of Forbidden Books in 1557, forbidding Catholics to read or even possess books written by certain authors. From the nineteenth century on the model for Catholic theology was a Roman theology based not on research or historical study of the received tradition but on authority; it was largely deductive and speculative, expressed in the categories of scholastic philosophy. By 1830 the word "magisterium" had become a term for the teaching office of bishops and popes exclusively. There were some bright moments in the subsequent history of Catholic theology that were more open to historical studies, for example John Henry Newman (1801–90) in England and theologians of the Tübingen School in Germany like Johann Sebastian von Drey (1777–1853) and Johann Adam Möhler (1796–1838). But if these and other nonscholastic Catholic theologians in the early nineteenth century were sensitive to the importance of history, tradition, and community, the Aristotelian neo-Thomists who populated the Roman schools were not.[14]

Leo XIII sought to recenter Catholic philosophy and theology on the thought of Aquinas with his encyclical *Aeterni Patris* (1879), but it was more a nineteenth-century neo-Thomism, hostile to modern philosophy and blind to the importance of history, not the thought of Aquinas himself. In the last two decades of the nineteenth century, professors in the Roman institutions "were seminary professors rather than creative philosophers and theologians.

12. See Gerhard Ebeling, *Word and Faith* (Philadelphia: Fortress, 1963), "The Meaning of 'Biblical Theology,'" 79–97.

13. Sandra M. Schneiders, *The Revelatory Text: Interpreting the New Testament as Sacred Scripture* (Collegeville, MN: Liturgical Press, 1999) 21–23.

14. See Gerald McCool, *Catholic Theology in the Nineteenth Century* (New York: Seabury Press, 1977) 13.

Their published works were basically school manuals whose purpose was the clear exposition of safe 'received' Thomistic doctrine rather than the stimulation of original thought."[15] With the campaign against modernism, launched in 1907 by Pius X with his encyclical *Pascendi dominici gregis* and the Holy Office's decree *Lamentabili sane*, Catholic theology was set back for another fifty years. Exemplified by the theological manuals or textbooks of the Roman schools, it remained heavily deductive, based on a scholastic theology that began from revealed first principles rather than being enriched by historical research.[16] As late as 1950, Pope Pius XII wrote in his encyclical *Humani generis* that the proper task of theologians was "to indicate for what reasons those things which are taught by the living magisterium are found in Holy Scripture and divine 'tradition,' whether explicitly or implicitly" (DS 3886). This suggests that the proper role of theologians was restricted to supplying arguments for the magisterium.

Historical Consciousness

Gradually, however, the church, awakening from its dogmatic slumber, came to accept a more historically conscious, critical theology.[17] The movement between 1930 and 1950 described by the French term *ressourcement* or "return" represented a return to the sources of the Catholic tradition in Scripture, the fathers of the church, and liturgy. The modern biblical movement studied biblical texts using historical-critical methods. The liturgical movement, retrieving the liturgical tradition of the church in the first millennium, sought to renew the church's liturgical life by encouraging a more active participation by the faithful. Though the Roman curia did not welcome these movements, Pope Pius XII gave them cautious encouragement in three important encyclicals. *Divino afflante Spiritu* (1943) allowed Catholic scholars to use modern historical-critical methods of biblical scholarship; *Mystici corporis* (1943), with its sacramental vision of the church as the body of Christ, had implications for the liturgical movement; while *Mediator Dei* (1947) gave the liturgical movement a cautious embrace.

In the 1950s the new interest in biblical, kerygmatic, and liturgical scholarship began to be felt beyond the seminary walls, though it was resisted by conservative scholars led by Monsignor Joseph Clifford Fenton, editor of

---

15. McCool, *Catholic Theology*, 238.

16. See Roger Haight, *Christian Community in History*, vol. 1, *Comparative Ecclesiology* (New York; Continuum, 2005) 308–10.

17. See Bernard J. F. Lonergan, "The Transition from a Classicist World View to Historical Mindedness," *A Second Collection*, ed. William F. J. Ryan and Bernard J. Tyrrell (London: Darton, Longman and Todd, 1974) 1–9.

the *American Ecclesiastical Review*.[18] By the end of the decade students in Catholic colleges began reading John L. McKenzie's *Two-Edged Sword: An Interpretation of the Old Testament* (1956), reflective of the new biblical scholarship, in addition to more traditional apologetic works by G. K. Chesterton and Frank Sheed.

The developments in Catholic theology in the years immediately prior to the council were to bear fruit at Vatican II. In its Constitution on the Church in the Modern World (*Gaudium et spes*) the council recognized the important role theology played in what is today called the dialogue with culture. Repeating Pope John XXIII's distinction between the truths of faith and the manner of expressing them, it encouraged theologians to develop new ways of communicating those truths, to find ways of incorporating the findings of the secular sciences, especially psychology and sociology, into the church's pastoral care. The constitution urged those doing theological studies in seminaries and universities to cooperate with scholars in other disciplines. It expressed the hope that more lay members of the church would receive an adequate theological formation and contribute to the discipline, anticipating the entrance of lay men and women into the field in the years that followed. Finally, it emphasized that theologians, both clerical and lay, should "be accorded a lawful freedom of inquiry, of thought, and of expression," tempered by humility and courage in their respective disciplines (GS 62). The note on freedom of inquiry was important. In the years before the council theologians such as Karl Rahner, Yves Congar, Henri de Lubac, Marie-Dominique Chenu, Teilhard de Chardin, and John Courtney Murray had been disciplined, dismissed from their positions, silenced, or forbidden to publish on certain topics, though the council was to vindicate their work.

After the council, theology began to show itself as a far more critical, interpretative discipline, reexamining the sources of theology, reinterpreting traditional formulas, and turning towards experience. The correlational method of David Tracy, which seeks to bring the two principal sources for theology, the Christian texts and common human experience and language, into a critical "correlation" would become extremely influential.[19] The changes taking place in the discipline would affect the way theology was taught in the universities. For example, when Gerard Sloyan became chair of the department of religious education at the Catholic University of America in 1957, without criticizing the formational aims of college theology, he began to stress historical-critical methods and specialization in the different

18. See Philip Gleason, *Contending with Modernity: Catholic Higher Education in the Twentieth Century* (New York: Oxford University Press, 1995) 302–04.

19. David Tracy, *Blessed Rage for Order* (New York: Seabury Press, 1975) 43–45.

theological disciplines. In 1958 Bernard Cooke, just returned from the Institut Catholique in Paris, began to reshape Marquette's undergraduate and graduate programs from a scholastic, manual approach to an emphasis on the historical and kerygmatic theology he had studied in Europe.[20]

From Clerical to Lay Profession

The traditional seminary locus for theological education meant that most lay men and especially women were excluded; theology was for priests. It was only in the mid-twentieth century that programs for higher studies in theology for the laity began to appear.

The Laicization of Theology

The first graduate program for women was established in 1943 when Sister Madeleva Wolff, C.S.C., began a School of Sacred Theology at St. Mary's College at Notre Dame, Indiana.[21] With Sister Madeleva's program as a model, Pope Pius XII in 1952 founded Regina Mundi, a pontifical institute in Rome to prepare women for teaching religion in Catholic women's colleges.[22] Lay men and women could do graduate work in Catholic theology faculties in Germany but were generally not admitted to doctoral studies, but in 1951 the Catholic faculty at the Munich's Ludwig-Maximilians Universität began admitting women to doctoral work. One of the first doctoral degrees awarded to a woman was given to Elisabeth Gössmann in 1954. Other universities in Germany and Austria opened their doors to lay men and women for doctoral studies at the end of the 1950s or early 1960s.

Marquette University was the first to make graduate education in theology available to laypeople in the United States. Its department of religion changed its name to theology in 1952; and in 1963, under the leadership of Bernard Cooke, Marquette began a doctoral program open to lay men and women, though it was called "religious studies," to head off possible objections from Rome. Other Catholic universities followed Marquette's lead. The School of Theology at the Catholic University of America began to admit women in 1966. As lay men and increasingly lay women completed their degrees and began moving into faculty positions in Catholic colleges and universities, the

---

20. Patrick W. Carey, "College Theology in Historical Perspective," in *American Catholic Traditions: Resources for Renewal*, ed. Sandra Yocum Mize and William Portier (Maryknoll, NY: Orbis Books, 1997) 259–60.

21. See M. Madeleva Wolff, *My First Seventy Years* (New York: Macmillan, 1959).

22. With the exclusion of women no longer a problem, Regina Mundi was closed in 2005.

locus of theological scholarship began to shift, from seminaries to universities and graduate schools.

At the same time, with new, professionally trained theologians taking teaching positions in Catholic colleges and universities, their departments began to professionalize. As they began to develop graduate programs in theology, their faculty members were increasingly expected to publish and to play an active role in the theological academy. The Catholic Theological Society of America, originally a society of seminary professors, began to accept their first lay members in 1965. The Society of Catholic College Teachers of Sacred Doctrine, founded in 1953, changed its name in 1967 to the College Theology Society.

By the 1970s undergraduate theology began to move in two directions. Some departments adopted the religious studies approach, others opted for theology proper. Some have combined both approaches. But as Patrick Carey observes, while practitioners of both approaches considered themselves rigorously academic, both also moved away from what were now considered the outdated pastoral functions of the college discipline. Bernard Cooke argued that deepening students' faith, promoting Christian behavior, and encouraging apostolic activities were not "proper academic objectives of theology," though as Carey points out, he did not abandon those goals completely.[23] But the future direction of the discipline had been established.

In 1967 the renamed College Theology Society identified itself as an ecumenical rather than simply a Catholic organization, and it endorsed a statement, "Religion as an Academic Discipline," issued by the Commission in Higher Education of the Association of American Colleges, stating that theology or religious studies departments were "designed to promote understanding of an important human concern rather than confessional commitment." As Carey notes, "Pastoral concerns, or concerns for the religious lives of the students, became an obsolete relic of a now defunct system."[24] By the late 1960s or early 1970s the number of courses required in theology or religious studies had been reduced considerably. Their purpose was seen as strictly academic. The students' religious life became the concern of newly established offices of campus ministry.

While the loss of a sense of pastoral responsibility in Catholic colleges and universities cannot be laid exclusively at the doors of their departments of theology or religious studies, they are sometimes part of the problem. The laicization of theology has meant that most theologians in Catholic

23. Carey, "College Theology in Historical Perspective," 261–262, at 262.
24. Ibid., citing Rosemary Rogers, "The Changing Concept of College Theology: A Case Study," a Ph.D. dissertation (Catholic University of America, 1973) 254.

colleges and universities see themselves primarily as academics. Many have been trained in non-Catholic institutions. As lay men and women, they are no longer subject to direct ecclesiastical authority as were their predecessors, who were priests or religious. The Vatican's recent efforts to call Catholic universities back to a stronger Catholic identity, and Catholic theologians to a more ecclesial sense of their vocation, has only served to make them nervous, if not hostile, towards what is seen by some as unwarranted interference of the church in their work.

Theologians and the Magisterium

From a Roman perspective, the laicization of theology meant that the Vatican had lost control over the practitioners of theology in the church. A number of recent documents have attempted to address this situation. In 1975 the Vatican's International Theological Commission (ITC) issued "Theses on the Relationship between the Ecclesial Magisterium and Theology." The document saw theologians as mediating between the magisterium and the People of God in two ways, communicating authentic teaching clearly and effectively, and giving expression to the insights of the baptized. Richard Gaillardetz says that in contrast to the descending, preconciliar model of the relationship, the document offered a cooperative, dialogical view.[25]

In 1989 the American bishops, working with the Catholic Theological Society of America, published a document called "Doctrinal Responsibility: Approaches to Promoting Cooperation and Resolving Misunderstandings between Bishops and Theologians." Drawing on the earlier ITC document, the bishops suggested guidelines for resolving differences.

In 1990 the Congregation for the Doctrine of the Faith published a document entitled "Instruction on the Ecclesial Vocation of the Theologian." It described the theologian's task as one of drawing "from the surrounding culture those elements which will allow him better to illumine one or other aspect of the mysteries of faith. This is certainly an arduous task that has its risks, but it is legitimate in itself and should be encouraged" (no. 10). Besides accepting with "theological faith" infallible pronouncements and teachings of the ordinary and universal magisterium proposed as divinely revealed, it added that truths concerning faith and morals, even if not divinely revealed, are nevertheless strictly and intimately connected with revelation and must

---

25. Richard R. Gaillardetz, *By What Authority? A Primer on Scripture, the Magisterium, and the Sense of the Faithful* (Collegeville, MN; Liturgical Press, 2003) 138; the document can be found in *Readings in Moral Theology*, no. 3, ed. Charles E. Curran and Richard A. McCormick (New York: Paulist Press, 1982) 151–70.

be firmly accepted and held when they are proposed "in a definitive way" (no. 23). Gaillardetz cites then-Cardinal Joseph Ratzinger, who pointed to a shift in the CDF document from a "'magisterium-theology' dualism" to a "triangular relationship: the People of God, as the bearer of the sense of faith and as the place common to all in the ensemble of faith, Magisterium and theology."[26]

Finally, on June 30, 1998, Pope John Paul II, in his apostolic letter "To Defend the Faith," inserted certain penalties into the Code of Canon Law for those who dissent from "definitive" but noninfallible teachings. In an accompanying commentary, Cardinal Ratzinger warned that those who dissent from truths such as these would be in a position of *"rejecting a truth of Catholic doctrine and would therefore no longer be in full communion with the Catholic Church."*[27] Among the theologians who have been disciplined or had their works questioned during the pontificates of John Paul II and Benedict XVI could be mentioned Charles Curran, Leonardo Boff, Gustavo Gutiérrez, Carmel McEnroy, Ivone Gebara, Tissa Balasuriya, Roger Haight, Jon Sobrino, Jacques Dupuis, and Peter Phan.[28]

The Mandatum

On August 15, 1990, Pope John Paul II promulgated his apostolic constitution on Catholic higher education, *Ex corde ecclesiae.*[29] Under discussion for a decade, the constitution had two major concerns, the religious identity of Catholic colleges and universities and their relationship to church authority. In its opening paragraph the pope played on the constitution's title, writing that a Catholic university "born from the heart of the church" is part of a tradition that can be traced back to the very origin of the university as an institution (no. 1). Drawing on his earlier experience as a university professor, he argued that in a Catholic university "research necessarily includes (a) the search for an integration of knowledge, (b) a dialogue between faith and reason, (c) an ethical concern, and (d) a theological perspective" (no. 15). All the university's activities—its teaching, scholarship, profes-

---

26. Gaillardetz, *By What Authority?* 139; Ratzinger's comments can be found in "Theology Is Not Private Idea of Theologian," *L'Osservatore Romano* [English ed.] 27 (July 2, 1990) 5.

27. John Paul II, *Ad tuendam fidem, Origins* 28/8 (1998) 112–16; Joseph Ratzinger, "Commentary on Profession of Faith's Concluding Paragraphs," *Origins* 28/8 (1998) 117, italics in original.

28. See Bradford Hinze, "A Decade of Disciplining Theologians," *Chicago Studies* 37/1 (Spring 2010), forthcoming.

29. *Origins* 20/17 (1990) 265–76.

sional training, and service—should be "connected with and in harmony with the evangelizing mission of the Church" (no. 49).

While most Catholic educators welcomed *Ex corde*'s call to renew the Catholic identity of their institutions, many raised objections to the accompanying "general norms" or ordinances to ensure the Catholic identity of the institutions and their fidelity to Catholic doctrine in their teaching. While Catholic educators had wanted consultation and dialogue, Rome wanted juridical norms. The most controversial of the general norms remains the requirement, in accordance with canon 812 of the 1983 Code of Canon Law, that Catholics who teach theological disciplines in Catholic colleges and universities receive a *mandatum* from "competent ecclesiastical authority," that is, the bishop or his delegate. The *mandatum* is defined as an acknowledgement that the professor teaches within the full communion of the Catholic Church. But once granted by authority, a *mandatum* can also be withdrawn. Many Catholic educators and theologians worry that this could jeopardize both the academic freedom of the theologian and the institutional autonomy of the university, or that those who refuse to seek it will be considered heterodox.

This is not to suggest that these departments are always beyond criticism. They who teach theology in Catholic universities should be concerned with handing on the Catholic tradition in its fullness and not just the latest theories of the academy. Their theology should be rooted in the life and faith of the church. When a position taken by a theologian is contrary to official Catholic teaching, the bishop has every right to say so publicly. But many question the need to add a further juridical relationship which could suggest episcopal interference in university matters. Ecclesial communion is far better served by relationships of mutual respect and collaboration.

Since the "Guidelines Concerning the Academic *Mandatum* in Catholic Universities (Canon 812)" were accepted for publication in June 2001,[30] the requirement for Catholic theologians to receive a *mandatum* has been resolved on local diocesan or archdiocesan levels. Some bishops, for example, Archbishop Elden Curtiss of Omaha, have ordered all faculty members to request and accept the *mandatum*, and have announced it publicly. In most other dioceses it has been granted quietly to those who asked for it, or identified themselves as Catholic theologians, though who has the *mandatum* is generally considered a private matter between the theologian and the bishop.

30. *Origins* 31/7 (2001) 128–31.

Undergraduate Theology Today

Departments of theology and religious studies in Catholic colleges and universities today are very different from the religion departments out of which they grew. First, in the attempt to be less confessional, many schools have opted for religious studies rather than theology, and are pluralistic in their offerings. Second, the departments themselves have become much more pluralistic; they are no longer mostly Catholic either in their student populations or in their faculties, and many of their professors have degrees from non-Catholic institutions. Third, the professionalization of theology has meant that many professors see themselves as responsible primarily to the academy, rather than to the church. In this section we will explore some of these issues.

Theology or Religious Studies?

As Catholic colleges and universities began to professionalize their religion departments in the years after Vatican II, many opted to establish departments of religious studies. It was only in 1972 that a major in religious studies was introduced at Loyola University of Los Angeles (now Loyola Marymount); in 1980 the name was changed to "Theology" and later to "Theological Studies." While scholars continue to disagree about the precise difference between theology and religious studies, it is generally agreed that theology involves a critical reflection on faith done from the perspective of that faith tradition itself, while religious studies is a nonconfessional, "objective" investigation of one or more religious traditions.[31] According to Thomas O'Meara, departments of religious studies exist mostly in the United States, sustained by the American separation of church and state. They are to be found most often in secular or non-church affiliated universities and offer courses generally detached from the faith, church, and religious life of the students.[32] Catholic universities more traditionally have theology departments.

Some departments in Catholic universities today carry both titles; they are departments of theology and religious studies. Catholic theologians like James Heft and Lawrence Cunningham, both of whom recognize the critical, ecumenical, and pluralistic nature of theology, make the case for theology

31. James L. Heft explores the debate over theology versus religious studies at some length in his "Theology's Place in a Catholic University," in *Theological Education in the Catholic Tradition*, ed. Patrick W. Carey and Earl C. Muller (New York: Crossroad, 1997) 195–201.

32. Thomas O'Meara, "The Department of Theology at a Catholic University," in *The Challenge and Promise of a Catholic University*, ed. Theodore M. Hesburgh (Notre Dame, IN: University of Notre Dame Press, 1994) 251.

departments in Catholic universities. For Heft it is a matter of preference, though more important to him is what the faculty actually do.[33] Cunningham suggests that "a theological faculty, dedicated to the Christian tradition in general and serious about its own denominational heritage in particular is an essential part of the self-identity of a denominational school."[34] O'Meara criticizes a contemporary Catholic department that would be "essentially" ecumenical without being mainly Catholic.[35]

The debate today is largely over nomenclature, as most Catholic theology departments, given their pluralism in courses and faculties, offer theology courses in the proper sense, courses in other religions which may or may not be taught by adherents of those religions, and courses that study religion from pluralistic religious, cultural, and sociological perspectives. But does theology in Catholic schools ground students in the Catholic intellectual tradition? As Melanie Morey and John Piderit point out in their study of Catholic higher education, administrators frequently refer to theology as the heart of the Catholic intellectual tradition on campus. Yet the required courses are minimal, generally only two courses, and "at many Catholic universities there is little Catholic content in many of the theology courses that are offered," so that many students graduate without being exposed to much Catholic theology, and few professors have either the time or the inclination to show how church teachings have an impact on other disciplines.[36]

Equally important is the question of *how* theology is done in Catholic universities. It must be more than a strictly academic pursuit. I once heard a Catholic professor remark, when asked how courses in the department of religious studies at his institution differed from those at a nearby state university, "ours are more academic."

A Catholic Department?

The days of a virtual minor in religion for every undergraduate at Catholic colleges and universities are long gone. Though a number of these institutions are in the process of developing new, more interdisciplinary core curriculums, the average theology or religious studies requirement today is two courses, as well as two courses in philosophy. Some institutions require a

33. Heft, "Theology's Place," 197.
34. Cited in Heft, "Theology's Place" 197; see Lawrence S. Cunningham, "Gladly Wolde He Lerne and Gladly Teche: The Catholic Scholar in the New Millennium," *The Cresset* (June 1992) 5.
35. Cited in Heft, "Theology's Place," 199.
36. Melanie M. Morey and John J. Piderit, *Catholic Higher Education: A Culture in Crisis* (Oxford: Oxford University Press, 2006) 106.

first theology course for all their students. But with little structure to the curriculum and a wide diversity of offerings, many students go through their undergraduate years without ever taking a course in the New Testament, Christology, the church, liturgy, or Christian ethics. Arguing that they have "had theology," many will take world religions and another course outside their own tradition, perhaps Buddhism or a course in theology and ecology. Thus they graduate without ever having read a gospel, studied Augustine, Aquinas, or Dorothy Day, or wrestled with contemporary social issues from a Catholic perspective. The increasing pluralism of Catholic theology departments, both in terms of their faculties and their courses, contributes to this lack of focus.

I remember once checking the list of theology courses at a very distinguished Jesuit university to see what was being offered that semester. There was an introduction to the Old Testament and a course on God. All other courses were special studies—feminist, gay, black, Latina/o, psychology and religion, comparative mythologies, or other religions. Nothing on ecclesiology, liturgy, Christology, pastoral theology, spirituality, Catholic social ethics, the Catholic tradition, or the sacraments—courses would one would presuppose to be prominent in a Catholic theology department. Some familiarity with Scripture should be essential. Lawrence Cunningham observes that from its beginnings theology has involved an encounter with Scripture; thus students should be introduced not just to methodology and exegesis, but also to the way exegesis interacts within the discipline of theology.[37]

A Strictly Academic Discipline?

In David Tracy's often-cited analysis, theologians have to address three different "publics" or communities: "the wider society, the academy and the church."[38] Today many theologians seem to have chosen to address chiefly the academy. This reflects in part the interests of the theologians as members of an academy who must publish in peer-reviewed journals for tenure and promotion and in part the changing nature of the discipline of academic theology itself. John C. Haughey describes how the objectives of theology "have changed from moral and religious formation through catechetics and apologetics to religious education to preparation for the lay apostolate to developing a critical capacity to reflect on faith." While he says a personal

37. Lawrence S. Cunningham, "The Undergraduate Theology Major," in *Theological Education in the Catholic Tradition*, ed. Patrick W. Carey and Earl C. Muller (New York: Crossroad, 1997) 101.
38. David Tracy, *The Analogical Imagination: Christian Theology and the Culture of Pluralism* (New York: Crossroad, 1986) 5.

appropriation of the Catholic faith seems to have been a constant through all these years, he acknowledges that today "it is not as clear that it is the faith of the Church that is being taught now as it is the faith of the teacher," which may or not be the Catholic faith.[39]

The separation of theology from a pastoral concern for the religious lives of the students in Catholic universities is usually justified with the argument that theologians are not concerned with "catechetics." While some theologians, in their concern to emphasize theology as a critical reflection on faith, exalt the catechist's role of instruction in the faith, many do not seem ready to acknowledge that the theologian has any responsibility for faith formation. According to Richard McBrien, the theologian "addresses the mature Christian" in the church and a wider audience beyond it, not all of them necessarily believers.[40] But while this is of course true, McBrien generally does not address the particular responsibilities of someone teaching undergraduate theology. The majority of undergraduates taking theology classes in Catholic colleges and universities today are virtually illiterate when it comes to an intellectual grasp of their faith. Nor are they yet really mature Christians. As Haughey argues,

> it is difficult to see how you can invite young people to reflect critically on a faith they either do not have or, having, do not know if they want to commit to. . . . Given this noncommittal context of the ordinary undergraduate, the pedagogical responsibilities of a faculty member would force him or her to function more like a religious educator than a theologian.[41]

James Heft observes that as a critical reflection on faith, "theology always has a catechetical component." Admitting that he has often heard faculty members in theology departments say that they do not "do catechetics," he suggests that they may be alluding with dismay to the religious illiteracy of their students. But he adds that if students cannot reflect critically on a faith of which they are ignorant, then "the faculty should provide supplemental instruction just as history and language professors do to get students up to speed in the discipline."[42]

Acknowledging that most undergraduates are not well informed in the specifics of Catholicism, Chester Gillis argues that it is not the university's

39. John C. Haughey, "Theology and the Mission of the Jesuit College and University," *Conversations* (Spring 1994) 6.

40. Richard P. McBrien, "What Is a Theologian?" *The Tidings* (April 26, 1996) 6.

41. Haughey, "Theology and the Mission," 10.

42. Heft, "Theology's Place in a Catholic University," 201.

job "to do remedial work."[43] Recently at my university one faculty member wanted to drop a description of our department's mission as having "a special emphasis on the service of the faith," arguing that our mission was education, not faith formation. One might ask, if the members of the theology department do not have a special responsibility for the service of the faith in a Catholic university, who then does? Such a responsibility cannot simply be shifted to campus ministry; as Haughey argues, "teaching must retain a pastoral side to it—and all the more so if the subject matter is faith and reflection thereon."[44] Still, few faculty members seem willing to recognize a responsibility for developing the religious or faith lives of their students.

It is not that they are necessarily hostile to the faith of the church, but not all have integrated their appreciation for theology's critical function with their own responsibilities as mediators of the tradition to their students. Some are more concerned with their research interests, and others are largely unconscious of their own objections to church authority and how it is used. Thus the academy wins out over the church. I have often seen books by members of the Jesus Seminar used as texts in first-year New Testament courses, including a book on Jesus by Burton Mack, the Seminar's most radical member who treats the Gospel of Mark as unhistorical, theological polemic. This was for students who were unfamiliar with basic Christology, most of whom had never read a gospel through from beginning to end, and were not exposed to other, more substantive texts.

If theology is more than a strictly academic discipline, then the ability of a perspective faculty member to serve the religious mission of the institution becomes increasingly important. Most Catholic universities today seek to address the sensitive question of "hiring for mission." That does not mean that a prospective faculty member has to be Catholic. But certainly they need to be men or women whose interests include more than the strictly professional. They must have at least a respect for the Catholic tradition and be able to buy into the university's mission and institutional identity. Even more, they should be able to serve it.

One perspective faculty member who was found acceptable for a position in theology, if not the first choice, said that his interest in theology was rooted in a desire to study religion to see how it had been used to "demonize" the other. This is not evidence of positive appreciation of religion in general, nor of Catholicism's importance in the university's mission. He saw religion as a type of pathology. As Peter Steinfels has written, "the place in hiring

---

43. Chester Gillis, "Complexities of Hiring for Mission," *Conversations* 34 (Fall 2008) 20.

44. Haughey, "Theology and the Mission," 7.

of religious commitment and religious interests and competencies in research and teaching must be confronted, and clear, meaningful policies
developed."[45]

Conclusion

Catholic colleges and universities before Vatican II were more concerned
with their students' religious and moral development than with helping them
learn how to think theologically. They took "religion" courses, apologetic
in nature, virtually every semester, as well as an equal number of courses in
scholastic philosophy. Attendance at Mass on Sundays and sometimes week-
days was required, as were weekend retreats. Morality was individualistic.
Instructors were almost exclusively priests and religious. John Haughey has
described this as a "custodial mode of operation."[46]

The situation today is very different. Theology has become a professional
discipline, taught by largely lay faculties, often trained in non-Catholic
graduate schools. Departments of theology or religious studies are pluralistic;
students read scholars from different Christian traditions and are introduced
to other world religions. But as a discipline, theology plays a small role in
the undergraduate curriculum. Most schools require no more than two
courses. Christian theology is only one option among many.

Some younger theologians today object that theology has become too
narrowly academic, unconcerned with the faith and life of the church.
Christopher Ruddy argues that too many theologians take the academy as
their primary model. They adopt its language of academic freedom but use
it negatively, in terms of freedom from interference rather than freedom for
inquiry and truth. Under pressure to publish in peer-reviewed journals, many
younger theologians are not able to contribute to the larger public debate in
the church. Too often their theology is "nonecclesial and irrelevant to the
needs of church and society."[47]

The question of Catholic identity remains an important one. Catholic
educators are well aware of the gradual secularization of the American
university system, built on the foundation of Protestant colleges such as
Harvard, Yale, Princeton, Dartmouth, Wellesley, Vassar, Smith, the University of Chicago, and the University of Southern California—to name just a

45. Peter Steinfels, *A People Adrift: The Crisis of the Roman Catholic Church in America*
(New York: Simon and Schuster, 2003) 176.
46. Haughey, "Theology and the Mission," 6.
47. Christopher Ruddy, "Young Theologians between a Rock and a Hard Place," *Commonweal* 37/8 (April 21, 2000) 17–18, at 18.

few. In his book *The Soul of the American University: From Protestant Establishment to Established Nonbelief*, George Marsden illustrates how these schools' insistence on moving beyond denominational or "confessional" identities to a "nonsectarian" religious universalism contributed "to the virtual exclusion of religious perspectives from the most influential centers of American intellectual life."[48]

Most Catholic educators today are concerned about the Catholic identity of their institutions, as we saw earlier. They have welcomed *Ex corde*'s emphasis on the importance of a strong Catholic identity, even if they remain uncomfortable with the attempt to define the relationship between Catholic institutions and the Catholic Church in juridical terms.

The challenge remains to host departments of theology and religious studies that are not just strongly Catholic, sufficiently pluralistic, and open their students to other faiths and religious traditions but that also exercise a care for handing on the faith of the church to succeeding generations. Many young adults have little knowledge of the Christian tradition and live in a consumer-driven culture in which religion becomes just once more choice.

At the same time, since the Second Vatican Council, Catholicism has recognized that faith and justice are inexorably conjoined, and so theological education also involves an education in the faith that does justice. Thus a crucial issue today is how to find ways to expand the walls of the classroom so that faith becomes a live option in a world where so many are marginalized and without hope. We will consider these issues in later chapters.

---

48. George Marsden, *The Soul of the American University: From Protestant Establishment to Established Nonbelief* (New York: Oxford University Press, 1994) 5.

Chapter 3

Education for Faith and Justice

When Pope John XXIII called the Catholic Church into council shortly after his election in 1958, he had a clear vision of what he wanted his council to accomplish. A month before it opened, he spoke of the need for the church to address issues of peace, the equality and rights of all peoples, the problems of underdeveloped countries, and the miseries faced by so many, and he suggested that the church be presented as "the Church of all, and *especially of the poor*."[1] The sixteen documents produced by the Second Vatican Council (1962–65) outlined the parameters for the renewal of Catholic faith and life.

Two constitutions focused on the church itself. The Dogmatic Constitution on the Church (*Lumen gentium*) looked inward, to the renewal of the church's self-understanding and its structures. The Pastoral Constitution on the Church in the Modern World (*Gaudium et spes*) sought to move the church away from the defensive posture it had assumed against the onslaughts of modernity and the secularism that followed in its wake, turning it towards the world in service. While the council did much to renew the church, few people realized how much it would change Catholic higher education as well.

The Church in the Modern World

In many ways *Gaudium et spes* can be seen as part Pope John XXIII's legacy. In a "Message to Humanity" nine days before the council opened, the Pope spoke of the church's concern for peace between peoples and for social justice: "As we undertake our work, therefore, we would emphasize whatever concerns the dignity of man, whatever contributes to a genuine

---

1. Cited by Peter Hebblethwaite, "John XXIII," in *Modern Catholicism: Vatican II and After*, ed. Adrian Hastings (New York: Oxford University Press, 1991) 30.

community of peoples." He quoted the first letter of John: "he who sees his brother in need and closes his heart against him, how does the love of God abide in him?"[2]

From its opening sentences, *Gaudium et spes* breathes this spirit of concern for the poor and disadvantaged:

> The joys and hopes, the grief and aguish of the people of our time, especially of those who are poor or afflicted, are the joys and hopes, the grief and anguish of the followers of Christ as well. Nothing that is genuinely human fails to find an echo in their hearts.[3]

No longer would the church be described as the "church militant," as though arrayed in battle lines against the world; it sought to be in solidarity with all peoples, especially with the poor.

The constitution describes the church as "reading the signs of the times," thus becoming aware of the transformations taking place in the world. While some enjoyed an abundance of wealth and economic well-being, others were plagued by hunger, need, and illiteracy. An unparalleled sense of freedom coexisted with new forms of social and psychological slavery. If the world was growing in interdependence, it was also fracturing into opposing camps. The results were new political, social, and economic divisions; racial and ideological antagonism; and the threat of total destruction (GS 4). The council fathers charted the changes brought on by industrialization, urbanization, socialization, and personalization (GS 6); they described the hungry crying out to their affluent neighbors, women claiming parity with men, laborers and agricultural workers insisting not just on the necessities of life but also on the opportunity to develop their talents and take an active part in economic, social, political, and cultural life (GS 9). It was to this world that the church sought to speak in the name of its Lord (GS 10).

Part 1 of the constitution underlines again the dignity of the human person, created "in the image of God," able to know and love their creator (GS 12). This foundational principle of Catholic social doctrine grounds its profound respect for human life, whether of the unborn, the elderly infirm, the poor or homeless, or the prisoner on death row.

Part 2, focusing on what it calls "Some More Urgent Problems," considers in separate chapters the dignity of marriage and the family; the proper development of culture, economic and social life; the political community;

---

2. Text in Walter M. Abbott, ed., *The Documents of Vatican II* (New York: America Press, 1966) 5.

3. GS 1; see *Vatican Council II: The Basic Sixteen Documents*, ed. Austin Flannery (New York: Costello Publishing Company, 1996) 163.

and the fostering of peace and a community of nations. Calling attention to contemporary social inequalities, among them contempt for the poor, the huge numbers of peoples deprived of the bare necessities of life, the growing contrast between economically more advanced countries and others with people living and working in conditions unworthy of human beings (GS 63), the chapter on economic life stresses that the ultimate purpose of economic production is not production, profit, or prestige but the service of humanity and therefore must be carried out so that God's design for humanity may be realized (GS 64). It also affirms the personal right to those in underdeveloped areas to emigrate (GS 65), an important point today, given the millions on the move, seeking better opportunities for their families.

The council also emphasized that the requirements of justice and equity call for serious efforts to address the immense economic inequalities which were increasing daily and which went hand in hand with individual and social discrimination. Those who come to other countries to find work, that is, immigrants, should be treated as persons, not just as instruments of production; public authorities should help them find decent housing, integrate them into the social life of the countries to which they come, and provide opportunities for technical and professional training. Each person has a right to work and deserves a dignified livelihood for themselves and their families. The laws of economics cannot be an excuse for ignoring the needs of persons and families (GS 67).

While the constitution affirms the right to private property, it stresses the social nature of the goods of the earth: "In their use of things people should regard the external good they lawfully possess as not just their own but common to others as well, in the sense that they can benefit others as well as themselves." But it also cites the traditional teaching of the fathers and doctors of the church that those "in extreme necessity are entitled to take what they need from the riches of others." It asks individuals and governments to remember the saying of the fathers: "Feed the people dying of hunger, because if you do not feed them you are killing them" (GS 69).

Running through the constitution like a leitmotif is the principle of the common good, another central value of Catholic social doctrine; it appears at least thirty times. Several times the constitution lifts up the rights of women. It recognizes the changing relationships between men and women (GS 8), including women's equity with men before the law (GS 9); rejects any discrimination based on sex, race, color, social conditions, language, culture, or religion; and affirms the rights of women to choose a husband, state of life, or to have the same access to educational or cultural benefits as men (GS 29) and to participate in cultural life (GS 60). It calls all people to "consider it their sacred duty to count social obligations among their chief duties today" (GS 30), thus moving beyond an individualistic morality, with the goal of working for a new communion of sisters and brothers among all who follow Christ in faith and love (GS 32).

It is also important to note the emphasis the constitution places on theology. Acknowledging that it is not always easy to reconcile culture with Christian thought, it encourages the faithful to work closely with their contemporaries in trying to understand their ways of thinking and feeling, and it calls on those teaching theology in seminaries and universities to cooperate with those in other disciplines, suggesting that there should be an interdisciplinary dimension to theology. It also expresses the hope that the laity receive adequate theological formation and be able to contribute to the advancement of the discipline. Importantly, it states that theological work for both laypeople and clerics calls for a "lawful freedom of inquiry, of thought, and of expression, tempered by humility and courage" (GS 62).

The Constitution on the Church in the Modern World is clearly prophetic, with its call for social justice, its concern for the rights of women, its positive appreciation of culture, its sense for what is now called globalization (cf. GS 54), and its recognition that social and economic inequities are a threat to peace. It was the inspiration for the liberation and feminist theologies that developed in the church after the council, and it led to a new commitment to justice on the part of Catholic religious orders and educational institutions.

Gaudium et spes was not without its faults. More emphasis on Jesus' preaching of the kingdom of God rather on the mediating function of the church might have helped it to develop a clearer vision.[4] Papal social encyclicals were often more explicit in developing principles for social justice. Joseph Ratzinger, a *peritus* at the council, objected to its pretheological concept of world, its emphasis on dialogue, and the "astonishing optimism" it displayed.[5]

Evangelization and Social Justice

But the constitution placed the social dimensions of the gospel at the center of the church's consciousness and would inspire many subsequent initiatives. It introduced a theme that would be repeatedly emphasized by the church's magisterium. At the 1971 Synod of Bishops, the bishops linked justice and evangelization in their document "Justice in the World": "Action

4. Enda McDonagh, "The Church in the Modern World (*Gaudium et spes*)," in *Modern Catholicism: Vatican II and After*, ed. Adrian Hastings (New York: Oxford University Press, 1991) 111.

5. See Joseph Ratzinger, *Principles of Catholic Theology: Building Stones for a Fundamental Theology* (San Francisco: Ignatius Press, 1987) 380.

on behalf of justice and participation in the transformation of the world fully appear to us as a constitutive dimension of the preaching of the Gospel, or, in other words, of the Church's mission for the redemption of the human race and its liberation from every oppressive situation" (no. 6).

Both Pope Paul VI and Pope John Paul II would continue to emphasize this theme. In his apostolic exhortation *Evangelii nuntiandi* (1975), Pope Paul VI argued that there were profound links between evangelization and liberation because the person "who is to be evangelized is not an abstract being but is subject to social and economic questions." One could not ignore "the importance of the problems so much discussed today, concerning justice, liberation, development and peace in the world. This would be to forget the lesson which comes to us from the Gospel concerning love of our neighbor who is suffering and in need" (no. 31). Similarly, Pope John Paul II would emphasize in his encyclical *Centesimus annus* (1991) that "to teach and to spread her social doctrine pertains to the Church's evangelizing mission and is an essential part of the Christian message" (no. 5). Thus evangelization can never be reduced to a narrow concern about the salvation of the individual; it includes the Gospel's message about liberation and reconciliation.

Pedro Arrupe

In the years that followed the council religious communities sought to renew their lives and their communities in light of the council's decrees. Jesuit father Pedro Arrupe was symbolic of a new generation of religious leaders. A Basque like St. Ignatius of Loyola (whom in a remarkable way he resembled), Arrupe was born in Bilbao, Spain, in 1907. He began his university education at the University of Madrid, but his medical studies were cut short when he entered the Society of Jesus in 1927. After ordination he continued his formation in the United States and Mexico before setting out for twenty-seven years in Japan as a missionary. This man, who experienced the most awesome destructive power of the twentieth century first-hand, was to give the Society of Jesus charismatic leadership and a new sense of direction.

On August 6, 1945, Arrupe was six kilometers from the center of Hiroshima when the atomic bomb was dropped on the city. Twelve hours after the bombing, he entered the stricken city which he described in a memoir as an "enormous lake of fire" and began tending survivors:[6]

6. *Recollections and Reflections of Pedro Arrupe*, S.J., trans. Yolanda T. De Mola (Wilmington: Michael Glazier, 1986) 24.

It was five in the afternoon. An indescribable spectacle met our gaze: a macabre vision which staggered the imagination. Before us lay a city completely destroyed. Through its streets we walked, stepping on ruins under which embers still felt warm. Any carelessness on our part could be fatal.

Much more terrible, however, was the tragic sight of those thousands of injured people begging for help. One such was a child who had a piece of glass imbedded in the pupil of his left eye, and another who had a large wooden splinter protruding like a dagger from between his ribs. Sobbing, he called out: "Father, save me!" Another victim was caught between two beams with his legs calcified up to his knees.[7]

At the Jesuits Thirty-First General Congregation in 1965, the year Vatican II concluded, Father Pedro Arrupe was elected Superior General. He was to lead the Society until 1981, when he suffered a stroke which left him paralyzed and debilitated until his death ten years later in 1991. He is considered by many Jesuits a second Ignatius and refounder of their order.

Men and Women for Others

On July 31, 1973, Father Arrupe spoke at the Tenth International Congress of Jesuit Alumni of Europe at Valencia, Spain. His talk, entitled "Men for Others," was addressed to a largely male audience; it has since been expanded to "Men and Women for Others," using language that has since become descriptive of the educational goals of Jesuit colleges and universities throughout the world.[8]

Arrupe begins by stating that education for justice has become in recent years one of the chief concerns of the church. Acknowledging that this had not previously been a focus of Jesuit education, he calls on Jesuit schools to take this up in a way equal to the demands of justice in the world. Such an interpretation of the "signs of the times," rooted in the Second Vatican Council, found echoes in papal encyclicals such as *Populorum progressio* (1967) and in the concerns of episcopal conferences in Latin America (1968), Africa (1969), Asia (1971), and particularly in the "Justice in the World" document of the 1971 Synod of Bishops mentioned earlier. While the mission of the church is not coextensive with the furthering of justice, it is as the synod teaches a *constitutive element* of that mission, an expression of the Gospel command to love God and our neighbor.

7. Ibid., 29.
8. http://www.creighton.edu/CollaborativeMinistry/men-for-others.html.

But "works of justice" cannot be understood in an individualistic sense. It means for Father Arrupe three things. First, it means an attitude of respect towards others which forbids ever using them as instruments for one's own profit. Second, it entails a firm resolve never to profit, even passively, from positions of power that derive from privilege. Third, it means not just a refusal to benefit from injustice but a counterattack against it, a decision to work with others to dismantle unjust social structures, to set free the weak, the oppressed, and the marginalized. Using language similar to that of liberation theology, he argues for personal conversion, but only as the beginning of a renewal or reform that reaches out to the periphery of our being, that is, to our habits, customs, patterns of thought, imagination, and will; it must be not only personal but social:

> For the structures of this world—our customs; our social, economic, and political systems; our commercial relations; in general, the institutions we have created for ourselves—insofar as they have injustice built into them, are the concrete forms in which sin is objectified. They are the consequences of our sins throughout history, as well as the continuing stimulus and spur for further sin.

Thus a new vision of justice calls for a new kind of spirituality, or an expansion of traditional spirituality and asceticism which is social as well as personal, since personal conversion can never be separated from structural social reform.

Father Arrupe's second line of reflection in the address concerns the formation of men and women who will advance the cause of justice in the modern world, the "men and women for others" needed by the church today who will help humanize the world and put it at the service of humankind. Their successes, however partial, are signs of the coming of the kingdom mysteriously among us. With love as the driving force, he encourages the cultivation of three attitudes: first, to love more simply, as individuals, families, and social groups, setting all these against the tide of a consumer society for the benefit of the majority of humankind; second, the firm determination not to profit from unjust sources, to reduce privilege for the sake of the underprivileged, the truly poor; and third, which he admits is the most difficult, the firm resolve to be agents of change, to actively undertake to reform unjust social structures. To form men and women for others becomes then the paramount objective of Jesuit education. "Only by being a man-or-woman-for-others does one become fully human, not only in the merely natural sense, but in the sense of being the 'spiritual' person of Saint Paul" filled with the Spirit of Christ. Today that is often expressed as the "faith that does justice."

The Thirty-Second General Congregation

In 1974, under Father Arrupe's leadership, representatives from Jesuit provinces around the world assembled for the Society's Thirty-Second General Congregation. Called together to reflect on the Society's ministries nine years after the close of Vatican II and after the cultural and social upheavals that followed in its wake, the congregation addressed a number of issues pertaining to the Society's life. Most significant was Decree 4, "Our Mission Today: The Service of Faith and the Promotion of Justice," which sought to reformulate the mission of the Society of Jesus for the contemporary world.[9]

The General Examen, written by Ignatius of Loyola about 1546 for his new religious order, described the mission of the Society of Jesus in the language of the sixteenth century. It strikes us today as somewhat individualistic:

> The end of this Society is to devote itself with God's grace not only to the salvation and perfection of the members' own souls, but also with that same grace to labor strenuously in giving aid towards the salvation and perfection of the souls of their fellowmen. (No. 3)

The Thirty-Second General Congregation translated that vision into language more reflective of the Society's self-understanding after the council. Decree 4 brought that language up-to-date:

> The mission of the Society of Jesus today is the service of faith, of which the promotion of justice is an absolute requirement. For reconciliation with God demands the reconciliation of people with one another. (No. 2)

In the years since this congregation, Jesuits throughout the world have struggled to integrate this emphasis on the service of faith and promotion of justice into their personal lives and their ministries, including into the programs of their colleges and universities. It has not been easy to do so. Not all have accepted the new emphasis on social justice. In Latin America it is often understood as implying a "preferential option for the poor." Others have been concerned lest this emphasis detract from the Society's traditional commitment to education and the intellectual life.

As Father Arrupe had predicted, the cost has been high. Since 1973, more than forty Jesuits have died because of their work for justice. Perhaps most dramatically, on November 16, 1989, soldiers from the Atlacatl Battalion, some of them trained at the School of the Americas in the United States,

---

9. See John W. Padberg, *Together in a Companionship: A History of the Thirty-First, Thirty-Second, and Thirty-Third General Congregations of the Society of Jesus* (St. Louis, MO: Institute of Jesuit Sources, 1994).

entered the Jesuit residence at the University of Central America in El Salvador, known popularly as the "UCA," dragged the six Jesuits living there outside and murdered them, along with their cook and her fifteen-year-old daughter. By this bloody act, the Salvadoran military wiped out almost the entire Jesuit leadership of the university.

Many have seen this emphasis on a faith that does justice as the Society's response to the council's call to "read the signs of the times" (GS 4), and other colleges and universities have embraced it as part of their mission. The Jesuits are not alone in suffering losses; many priests, brothers, and nuns have been killed, as well as thousands of lay men and women.[10]

Proyección Social

One of the most insightful advances on the idea of a Christian university since Cardinal John Henry Newman comes from the Jesuits of El Salvador, working at the University of Central America.[11] Among them, Ignacio Ellacuría, Jon Sobrino, and Dean Brackley stand out. Ellacuría, greatly influenced by the Spanish philosopher Xavier Zubiri and his own experience in El Salvador, reformulated the goals of Catholic higher education; Sobrino, writing from the perspective of a theology of liberation, provided the theological foundation; and Brackley has popularized their vision, expressing it in terms of seven standards. Under their influence, the UCA's educational philosophy and vision were rearticulated from the perspective of the option for the poor.

Ignacio Ellacuría

The UCA's president and one of the six Jesuits assassinated by Salvadoran troops on November 16, 1989, Father Ellacuría was an original thinker in his own right. Born November 9, 1930, in the Basque country of Spain, he entered the Jesuits at Loyola in 1947 and moved to El Salvador a year later with five other novices. In the following years he studied at Quito in Ecuador (1950–55), at Innsbruck in Austria (1958–62) under Karl Rahner, and at Madrid in Spain (1962–67), where he completed a dissertation on Zubiri under a director from the university but with the philosopher's personal assistance. Ellacuría's magnum opus, *Philosophy of Historical Reality*, published posthumously, was indebted to Zubiri. But while Zubiri's focus was on the unity of the

---

10. See Penny Lernoux, *Cry of the People: The Struggle for Human Rights in Latin America* (New York: Penguin Books, 1982).

11. This is the thesis of Jon Sobrino in his *Companions of Jesus: The Jesuit Martyrs of El Salvador* (Maryknoll, NY: Orbis Books, 1990) 38.

material cosmos, including its personal and social dimensions, Ellacuría's concern, reflecting his own work in philosophy and theology, was historical reality, specifically that of Latin America and what he called, using one of his favorite metaphors, its "crucified people."[12]

> It is this move [beyond Zubiri and Rahner] that allows him to treat the "option for the poor" made by the church in Latin America as a "concrete universal," (in Rahner's sense of the term) of significance for the whole church. It also grounds his prophetic cry that the "crucified people" of the Third World constitute the "principle [sic] . . . sign of the times" orienting the "universal historical mission" of the church in the world today.[13]

Beyond his European mentors, Ellacuría's thought was shaped by the theology of liberation, the call of the Latin American bishops at Medellín (1968) to commit to an "option for the poor," the spirituality of the Spiritual Exercises, particularly by a retreat the Jesuits of Central America made in 1969 as they attempted to respond to the Second Vatican Council, and perhaps most of all by the example of Archbishop Oscar Romero. In Sobrino's words, "the UCA learned how to fulfill its mission as a Christian university by watching what it meant to run the Archdiocese from the perspective of solidarity with the poor."[14]

Under Ellacuría's influence, first as a board member (1967–89) and then as president (1979–89), the UCA underwent a dramatic change to reflect the *realidad* of Central America. In his history of the UCA, Román Mayorga points to 1972 as the key year. A project for refocusing the university's mission was initiated, which resulted in an "Organizational Handbook of the University."[15] The handbook outlined a structure for addressing the national reality of El Salvador through the university's teaching, research, and "social outreach," described by the Spanish term *proyección social*.[16] Ellacuría defined *proyección social* as "the primordial function of the UCA, that from

12. Ignacio Ellacuría, *Filosofía de la realidad histórica* (San Salvador: UCA Editores, 1990).

13. Robert Lassalle-Klein, "Introduction," in Kevin F. Burke and Robert Lassalle-Klein, *Love that Produces Hope: The Thought of Ignacio Ellacuría* (Collegeville, MN: Liturgical Press, 2006) xxv.

14. Ibid., xxv–vi.

15. Román Mayorga, *La Universidad Para El Cambio Social* (San Salvador: UCA Editores, 1976) 44–46; see also Charles J. Beirne, *Jesuit Education and Social Change in El Salvador* (New York: Garland Publishing, 1996); Beirne traces the history of the UCA through the Ellacuría years (1979–89), detailing the challenges from external forces as well as some at the university and in the hierarchy of the Church.

16. Mayorga, ibid., 213; Mayorga includes important sections of the handbook, entitled "Manual de Organizacion de la Universidad," in his history, 212–24.

which it receives its totality as a university, and from which all its activities receive their overall orientation. This orientation must be translated into practical measures [social outreach programs] effective in themselves and present and operative in the totality of all UCA functions."[17] It described the university's efforts to influence society directly, helping to shape the collective consciousness of the country through its analysis and its media, allowing the concrete cries of the oppressed majority to resonate through them.[18] Thus in 1985 Segundo Montes founded the Human Rights Institute at the UCA and a year later Ignacio Martín-Baró established the University Institute for Public Opinion, both of which would document and publicize the sufferings of El Salvador's peoples as well as U.S. silence about violations of human rights by the government of El Salvador which it supported.

The university's charter document, published in May 1979, insists that "the UCA seeks to be an institutional university response to the historical reality of the country, considered from an ethical perspective as an unjust and irrational reality that should be transformed. . . . It does this in a university manner and . . . with a Christian inspiration."[19] The idea was to make the university function as a critical conscience, able to speak to its society, to analyze it and its efforts to reform in light of Catholic social teaching, the Gospel teaching on the kingdom of God, and the option for the poor, thus historicizing the activities of the university.[20]

Ellacuría had to spend seventeen months of his first thirty-six-month term as president in exile (1980–82) because of threats against his life. In June 1982, two years after Romero's murder, he gave the commencement address at Santa Clara University. Recalling that the UCA, officially known as the *Universidad Centroamerica José Simeon Cañas*, bore the name of a Salvadoran priest who as a congressman moved the Constitutional Assembly in 1824 to abolish slavery in Central America, he argued that there are two aspects to every university. First, it deals with culture, with knowledge, the use of the intellect. Thus, it must be an institution that is both academically excellent and ethically oriented. Second, it must be concerned with social

17. Beirne, *Jesuit Education and Social Change*, 175.

18. See Ignacio Ellacuría, "Is a Different Kind of University Possible?" in *Towards a Society that Serves its People: the Intellectual Contribution of El Salvador's Murdered Jesuits*, ed. John Hassett and Hugh Lacey (Washington, DC: Georgetown University Press, 1991) 203.

19. Cited by Burke and Lassalle-Klein, *Love that Produces Hope*, 106; see Ellacuría, "Las funciones fundamentales de la universidad y su operativizacion," in *Planteamiento Universitario 1989* (San Salvador: UCA Editores, 1989) 47; first published 1979.

20. Ellacuría, "Las funciones fundamentals," 53.

reality, precisely because as a university it is inescapably a social force. It must transform and enlighten the society in which it lives.[21]

How does a university do this? It must use all the means at its disposal. As an intellectual community, it must analyze causes, use imagination and creativity to discover remedies, communicate a consciousness that inspires its constituencies, educate professionals with a conscience who will become the immediate instruments of transformation, and develop an educational institution that is both academically excellent and ethically oriented. Sobrino has spoken of Ellacuría's thought on the idea of a Christian university as comparable in importance to that of Cardinal Newman.[22] While Newman saw the cultivation of knowledge for its own sake as part of the work of a university, Ellacuría emphasized the option for the poor in Catholic social teaching, linking the university to the vision of St. Ignatius in the Spiritual Exercises: "ask yourselves the three questions Ignatius of Loyola put to himself as he stood in front of a crucified world: What have I done for Christ in this world? What am I doing now? And above all, what should I do? The answers lie both in your academic responsibility and in your personal responsibility."[23]

Jon Sobrino

Jon Sobrino was born into a Basque family in Barcelona in 1938; like Ellacuría, he also went to El Salvador while still a novice, though ten years later than Ellacuría. With a doctorate in theology from Sankt Georgen, the Jesuit Hochschule in Frankfurt, Germany, Sobrino is well known for his works on the theology of liberation. A member of Ellacuría's community at the UCA, Sobrino narrowly escaped death, as he was in Thailand the night his companions were killed.

Influenced by Jürgen Moltmann's concept of a "crucified God" and Ellacuría's emphasis on the "crucified people" as a "sign of the times," Sobrino insists that experience of the poor must be the central context for theology today.[24] In a deliberately provocative essay entitled *Extra pauperes nulla salus* (no salvation outside the poor), he first catalogs the inequities of the modern world—the dehumanizing poverty, violence, and suffering of so many, the

---

21. Ignacio Ellacuría, "The Task of a Christian University," in Jon Sobrino, *Companions of Jesus: The Jesuit Martyrs of El Salvador* (Maryknoll, NY: Orbis Books, 1990) 149.

22. Sobrino, *Companions of Jesus*, 38.

23. Ellacuría, "The Task of a Christian University," in Sobrino, *Companions of Jesus*, 151.

24. Jon Sobrino, *No Salvation Outside the Poor: Prophetic-Utopian Essays* (Maryknoll, NY: Orbis Books, 2008) 3–8; see also Robert Lassalle-Klein, "Jesus of Galilee and the Crucified People: The Contextual Christology of Jon Sobrino and Ignacio Ellacuría," *Theological Studies* 70/2 (2009) 347–76.

rape of women, the enormous amounts of money spent on arms, the ravages of diseases like AIDS and malaria, or simple lack of food and drinking water— and then calls for a mystagogy which understands salvation in relation to the poor.[25] It is not that the poor are themselves innocent; both the *mysterium salutis* and the *mysterium iniquitatis* can be discerned among them as among others. But the poor for Sobrino are bearers of truth. "By virtue of what they are, they offer light to the world of abundance, so that this world might see its own truth and thus be able to move towards all truth."[26]

In an article exploring whether a Christian university is really possible, Sobrino argues that a university's identity is not established simply by de-claring itself Christian; it comes from being at the service of the kingdom of God, taking an option for the poor.[27] Because a university is incarnated in a social reality that gives it power—economic, political, and religious power—it can easily become disincarnated from the social reality of the majority of the world which is poor and marginalized.

Nor does its commitment to education, its Christian formation of university members, or its theological activity in itself make a university Christian. Theology can easily become disconnected from its roots in history and in the real hopes of the poor. Its concern is not to defend truth accepted a priori but rather to help society grow in the direction of the kingdom of God. Education can be narrow or professional, failing to form students against the horizon of social reality, and its graduates for the most part reinforce those very social systems that disadvantage the poor. Christian formation is measured not by religious practice but by service towards a more human society.

Sobrino articulates two principles for a Christian university. First, the kingdom of God should function as horizon and finality for the university's endeavors. Proclaiming the kingdom means a practical demand to make it happen. Second, the option for the poor does not mean necessarily physical or geographical location among the poor or changing the makeup of the university's student body but finding ways to bring the world of the poor into the university so that students learn to see the world from their point of view. It should also inform the way the university's intellectual resources are utilized, focusing on the underside of history, letting the poor become a *locus theologicus*, a place for discerning God's active presence. At the end of his essay, he turns like Ellacuría to the Spiritual Exercises, asking with

25. Ibid., 49; the phrase *extra paupers nulla salus* is not original to Sobrino; he traces antecedents in the thought of Edward Schillebeeckx and found the phrase itself in the work of a graduate student (70–71).

26. Ibid., 60.

27. Sobrino, "The University's Christian Inspiration," in *Companions of Jesus*, 152.

St. Ignatius, what have we done and what are we going to do for the Cruci-fied, adding "and for the crucified peoples?"[28]

The Vatican's Congregation for the Doctrine of the Faith has found Sobrino's Christology problematic. It charges that he identifies the "ecclesial setting" for Christology with the church of the poor, claiming that this func-tions in his work as an alternative "ecclesial foundation" to the apostolic faith transmitted through the church for all generations (no. 2), and that he separates the kingdom of God from Jesus himself (no. 7).[29] But Sobrino has his own problems with the preparatory documents for the Fifth Latin Ameri-can Bishops' Conference meeting in Aparecida, Brazil, (May 2007), criticiz-ing it for substituting an abstract Christ for the concrete Jesus of Nazareth, resulting in what he calls "an eclipse of the kingdom of God."[30]

Dean Brackley

Born in upstate New York, Dean Brackley entered the Society of Jesus in 1964 and received a doctorate in theological ethics from the University of Chicago in 1980. Long involved in social justice ministries, he was one of five Jesuits who took the place of the six Jesuits murdered at the UCA in 1989. Like Ellacuría and Sobrino, Brackley has argued for a transformation of Catholic higher education to better serve the church's commitment to social justice.

Brackley argues that Catholic colleges and universities have a unique role to play precisely as Catholic; they cannot measure their academic excellence by the same yardstick as other universities such as Harvard or Stanford, nor can they turn in on themselves as confessional enclaves. His particular contribution has been to spell out what he calls seven "higher standards" for Catholic higher education.[31] I will try to summarize them briefly here.

1. *Understand the real world.* Appealing to the thought of Ignacio Ellacuría, Brackley insists that the primary object of university study should be *reality,* that is, the real world in all its concrete, social, and existential dimensions. He is not against the traditional focus on the arts in Catholic education, though he does raise critical questions about

---

28. Ibid., 172.

29. See Congregation for the Doctrine of the Faith, "Notification on the Works of Father Jon Sobrino, S.J.," November 26, 2006; also William P. Loewe, "The Sobrino File: How to Read the Vatican's Latest notification," *Commonweal* 134/10 (March 18, 2007).

30. Jon Sobrino, "The Centrality of the Kingdom of God Announced by Jesus," in *No Salvation Outside the Poor*, 77.

31. Dean Brackley, "Higher Standards" in *A Jesuit Education Reader*, ed. George W. Traub (Chicago: Loyola Press, 2008) 189–94.

the too-frequent reduction of the undergraduate curriculum to narrow subspecialties. But what is most problematic for him is that so many students graduate from Catholic universities with little understanding of the concrete problems faced by real people, among them homelessness, abortion, or their own country's military adventures, and he remarks on their "striking level of ignorance" when it comes to vital political issues. Education should deal with reality.

2. *Focus on the big questions.* Closely related to the first, the second standard is more specifically Christian. If in the language of faith, the cross of Jesus stands as the center of reality, then education must address those questions that concern the drama of life and death, justice and liberation, good and evil, grace and sin. Its goal must be not just the imparting of information but the acquiring of wisdom.

3. *Free us from bias.* Seeking truth, always the goal of a humanistic education, means uncovering the hidden interests that come from unexamined assumptions, class interests, or simple ignorance. It requires a reason that is not just theoretical but rooted in experience and practice, nourished by contemplation, affectivity, and imagination. Thus Brackley calls for a "cognitive liberation" that requires personal change.

> We need wholesome crises to help expand our horizons. Frequently, such experiences occur when students engage in activities, like service learning, that draw them into close contact with poverty and suffering. There they are mugged by reality. The humanity of the people they encounter, some of them victims of injustice, crashes through students' defenses, provoking a salutary disorientation, much like the experience of falling in love.[32]

This is especially necessary for the middle-class "tribe" to which so many of our students belong.

4. *Help students discover their vocation.* With so many contradictory role models before them, everyone from Mother Teresa to Britney Spears, and with so much pressure from a consumerist culture that stresses getting and spending, students need help to discover their own unique vocations, rooted ultimately in the call of Christ. Brackley quotes the words of Ita Ford, martyred in El Salvador in 1980, to her young niece: "I hope you come to find that which gives life a deep meaning for you. Something worth living for—maybe even worth dying for—something that energizes you, enthuses you, enables you to keep moving ahead."[33]

---

32. Brackley, "Higher Standards," 191.
33. Ibid., 192.

5. *Economic diversity*. The diversity so celebrated today must include economic diversity, so that higher education is not just based on wealth or privilege. Brackley is not naive about the financial challenges of running a university, but he also comments on the first-rate athletic facilities and other amenities which can foster an upscale consumer culture on campus. He makes three suggestions: promote a culture of simplicity, maximize scholarship based on need rather than athletic or scholastic ability, and include fifty million dollars for scholarships in the next capital campaign.

6. *Truth in advertising*. Catholic colleges and universities should welcome those of other faiths and no faith, but they should also be truly Catholic, places where the Catholic tradition is studied, debated, and handed on. "We should fear for the future if students are graduating with first-class training in, say, economics and only a First Communion or a Newsweek understanding of the faith."[34]

7. *Speak to the wider world*. Here Brackley introduces the concept of *proyección social* or social outreach to "include all those means by which the university communicates, or projects, social criticism and constructive proposals beyond the campus into the wider society."[35] *Proyección social* asks that all the research and communication faculties of the university turn outward to reflect the social reality in which the university is situated to the wider community. He acknowledges that this can be risky—indeed, the UCA paid a heavy price for reflecting the reality of Salvadoran society outward, as we have seen—but it also can serve a much stronger sense of institutional identity and mission.

A North American Context

Catholic higher education in the United States cannot simply adopt the Central American model. Not only are our institutions very different but so are the social conditions. Still, there is much to be learned from the emphasis of the Jesuits in Central America. We have focused on them because of their serious and costly effort to rethink Catholic higher education in a way rooted in the Gospel.

But they are not alone. Many theologians in the United States today are stressing doing and teaching theology in the context of the poor, and Catholic colleges and universities are placing considerable emphasis on service learning and others types of courses that stress experience. Paul Fitzgerald notes

34. Ibid., 193.
35. Ibid., 194.

that when students study Catholic social doctrine from within specific contexts of marginalization and suffering, it often becomes compelling for them.[36] William O'Neill speaks of the "epistemic or hermeneutical privilege" of the poor which "emerges as a touchstone of the legitimacy of our prevailing institutional arrangements; only thus can we offer an equitable assessment of our legal enactments, juridical decisions, economic policies, etc."[37] Building on the work of Gustavo Gutiérrez, Roberto Goizueta argues for the recovery of lived faith of the people, especially the poor, with a praxis rooted in God's word. Without this, theology falls into the modernist and postmodernist trap of privileging the immaterial and abstract over the material and concrete. "Thus, rather than understanding the construction of meaning as necessarily linked to the disclosure of truth, to revelation, truth-as-disclosed is simply reduced to meaning-as-constructed."[38]

Service learning should be distinguished from the many forms of volunteerism by linking it to the rigorous intellectual discipline of an academic course. The PULSE Program for Service Learning at Boston College offers a twelve-credit, two-semester course, Personal and Social Responsibility, which fulfills the core requirement for both philosophy and theology; it combines academic work, community service, and student reflection. Gonzaga University offers between fifty and ninety service-learning courses every semester. The University of Notre Dame requires a one-unit course on Catholic social teaching before students go on semester break or summer immersion course; for a semester-long immersion experience a three-unit course is a prerequisite. Approximately 10 percent of Notre Dame's graduating class commits to at least a year of full-time service in the United States or abroad.

Conclusion

If Catholic higher education is to reach young people today, it must address the real problems of the world in which we live. Justice, with its concern for the disadvantaged and the suffering, must be central. In a talk at Santa Clara University in 2000, Father General Peter-Hans Kolvenbach stressed the importance of direct service to the poor and the disadvantaged:

36. See Paul Fitzgerald, "Doing Theology in the City," *Cross Currents* 51 (Spring 2001).

37. William O'Neill, "No Amnesty for Sorrow: The Privilege of the Poor in Christian Social Ethics," *Theological Studies* 55 (1994) 648.

38. Roberto Goizueta, "A Ressourcement from the Margins: U.S. Popular Catholicism as Lived Religion," in *Theology and Lived Christianity*, ed. David Hammond, Annual Publication of the College Theology Society, vol. 45 (Mystic, CN: Twenty-Third Publications/Bayard, 2000) 4–10, at 8.

Our students are involved in every sort of social action—tutoring drop-outs, demonstrating in Seattle, serving in soup kitchens, promoting pro-life, protesting against the School of the Americas—and we are proud of them for it. But the real measure of our Jesuit universities lies in who our students become. . . . We must therefore raise our Jesuit educational standard to "educate the whole person of solidarity for the real world." Solidarity is learned through "contact" rather than through "concepts." . . . When the heart is touched by direct experience, the mind may be challenged to change.[39]

But Catholic higher education cannot be reduced simply to a concern for justice. Catholic schools are not alone in addressing social issues. As Melanie Morey and John Piderit have pointed out, "Social justice, in fact, stirs great interest not just in Catholic colleges and universities but in American universities across the spectrum. Most four-year colleges—be they public or private, sectarian or nonsectarian—have extensive programs emphasizing service and justice. . . . Indeed, many nonsectarian institutions have programs that are more extensive than those at similarly sized Catholic institutions."[40]

Catholic higher education is concerned fundamentally with the human in all its dimensions, its highest achievements, its contemporary suffering, and the faith that gives it meaning. With its origin in the medieval universities and the Jesuit network of schools in the seventeenth and eighteenth centuries, Catholic higher education from the beginning has been founded on the humanities, with their liberating, humanizing potential, seeking a deeper understanding of human persons in their many-faceted reality—interpersonal, social, creative, political, economic, and religious. Thus Catholic higher education aims at the education and transformation of the individual. Jesuit schools express this by speaking of the service of faith, the promotion of justice, forming men and women for others, and what they call *cura personalis*, meaning a care for each student in his or her uniqueness.

But in all this, the *humanum* must be understood from a perspective illuminated by Christian faith, with the vision of the cross and resurrection of Jesus at its center. It is this vision, founded on Christian faith, rooted in the preaching of the historical Jesus, which must be the unifying principle of Catholic higher education.

Of course, not all in our university community share in a specifically Christian vision, though many buy into and support the university's mission. A university which is truly Catholic is also pluralistic; it must always make

39. Peter-Hans Kolvenbach, "As I See It," Santa Clara University (October 6, 2000).
40. Melanie M. Morey and John J. Piderit, *Catholic Higher Education: A Culture in Crisis* (Oxford: Oxford University Press, 2006) 57.

those who come from other faith traditions or those without a specific faith welcome. As the Thirty-Fourth General Congregation said in its Decree on Interreligious Dialogue, "to be religious today is to be interreligious in the sense that a positive relationship with believers of other faiths is a requirement in a world of religious pluralism."[41]

But the Christian faith, mediated by the Catholic tradition, must have a privileged place in the university, not just in theology and campus ministry, but in the curriculum and the educational work of the various departments and divisions of the university.

The dynamic structure of human understanding, which moves from experience to understanding and ultimately to judgment which grounds action, suggests that service learning, immersion experiences, and opportunities to live among the poor in countries different from our own should play an important role in Catholic higher education today. Theological education in Catholic universities in particular should stress praxis, with its experiential component. Such an emphasis is important, not just because it enables students and the university to serve the world in its needs, but also because it serves "the faith of the practitioner, the faith of which *praxis* is a constitutive moment."[42] Thus education for both faith and justice are controlling values.

In the next chapter we will ask the question, who are the students who come to our universities today?

41. *Documents of the Thirty-Fourth General Congregation of the Society of Jesus* (St. Louis: Institute of Jesuit Sources, 1995), "Our Mission and Interreligious Dialogue," no. 3.

42. Paul G. Crowley, "Theology in the Jesuit University," in *The Jesuit Tradition in Education and Mission: A 450-Year Perspective*, ed. Christopher Chapple (Scranton: University of Scranton Press, 1993) 162–63, at 163.

——————— Chapter 4 ———————

Young Adult Catholics Today

So who are the young people who come to Catholic colleges and universities today? Are they well informed about their faith? Are they committed to their church, willing to take up active roles within it? Are they ready to take their place as leaders in the church of tomorrow? Religious sociologist Robert Wuthnow argues that "unless religious leaders take younger adults more seriously, the future of American religion is in doubt."[1]

A number of recent sociological surveys on young adult Catholics and religious practice in the United States today have brought less-than-encouraging news. The first is a study conducted by two researchers at the University of North Carolina in Chapel Hill entitled *Soul Searching: The Religious and Spiritual Lives of American Teenagers*. The second, *American Catholics Today*, by William D'Antonio and associates, is the fourth in a series of studies on American Catholics. The third is the Pew Forum on Religion and Public Life's "U.S. Religious Landscape Survey" (February 25, 2008).

Two other studies are more encouraging. One is Tim Muldoon's *Seeds of Hope: Young Adults and the Catholic Church in the United States*. The other is the "Young Adult Catholics and Their Future in Ministry" report, commissioned by the Lilly Endowment–funded Emerging Models of Pastoral Leadership Project. We will consider these five reports briefly before examining some of their implications, particularly as they give a picture of young Catholics today. After drawing some initial conclusions from the data, I will suggest some strategies for engaging young adults more actively in the life and mission of the church.

---

1. Rubert Wuthnow, *After the Baby Boomers: How Twenty- and Thirty-Somethings Are Shaping the Future of American Religion* (Princeton, NJ: Princeton University Press, 2007) 17.

The Data

1. The North Carolina Study (2005)

Soul Searching, the North Carolina study, reported that U.S. Catholic teenagers are behind their Protestant peers—sometimes by as much as 25 percentage points—in terms of standards of religious belief, practice, and commitments. Indeed, many of them are "living far outside of official Church norms defining true Catholic faithfulness."[2] Comparing Catholic teenagers to cohorts of Protestant teens—mainline, conservative, and black—the researchers found that only 10 percent of Catholic teenagers said religion was "extremely important" in shaping their daily lives, compared to 20, 29, and 31 percent respectively for the other groups.[3]

The lower scores for Catholic teenagers so impressed the researchers that they devoted a separate chapter to them. In their conclusions they emphasized the importance of parents in the religious and spiritual lives of their children; the best rule of thumb for adults thinking about the "faith outcome" of their children is the rule, "We'll get what we are."[4] They believe that "the evidence clearly shows that [the] single most important social influence on the religious and spiritual lives of adolescents is their parents."[5] They also observed that the Catholic Church needs to "invest a great deal more attention, creativity, and institutional resources into its young members—and therefore into its own life."[6]

2. The D'Antonio Survey (2007)

The D'Antonio survey, *American Catholics Today,* reports that the level of church commitment on the part of Catholics has continued to decline.[7] Young adult Catholics are the least committed; they are only "loosely tethered to the Church."

> Barely half say they would never leave the Church. Only four in ten say the Church is the most important part—or one of the most important parts—of their lives. Only one-fourth go to Mass on a weekly basis. Less

2. Christian Smith and Melinda Lundquist Denton, *Soul Searching: The Religious and Spiritual Lives of American Teenagers* (New York: Oxford University Press, 2005) 194.

3. Ibid., 40.

4. Ibid., 216.

5. Ibid., 261.

6. Ibid., 217.

7. William D'Antonio, James D. Davidson, Dean R. Hoge, and Mary L. Gautier, *American Catholics Today: New Realities of their Faith and their Church* (New York: Rowman and Littlefield, 2007) 47.

than half believe that the teaching authority claimed by the Vatican is very important. A majority disagree with Church teachings related to sexual and reproductive issues, such as birth control and abortion.[8]

As William Dinges argues, the religious individualism described in the D'Antonio survey is "linked with autonomy in the moral realm; with the diminution or rejection of ecclesial authority; with more direct access to the sacred; with a higher priority for personal spiritual fulfillment; and with a privatized spirituality only loosely connected with established traditions."[9]

I made similar observations in *Being Catholic in a Culture of Choice*. There I argued that the majority of young adult Catholics have a diminished Catholic identity, a selective approach to authority, and a decreased or "thin" commitment to the institutional church.[10] The D'Antonio study nuances this somewhat; they point out two things they learned about the relationship between Catholic identity and commitment to the church. "First, identity is positively correlated with commitment. It contributes to and is reinforced by commitment to the Church. Second, although the two overlap, there are still some important differences between them. Catholics are more highly aligned with the faith than they are attached to the Church."[11]

At the same time, there is considerable evidence of another, smaller group of young Catholics that should not be ignored, a significant minority who are more passionate about their faith, more ecclesial in its expression, and more concerned with their identity precisely as Catholic Christians.[12] Though James Davidson and Dean Hoge in their earlier works said that they found no evidence that young Catholics were moving in a more traditional direction, *American Catholics Today* acknowledges this minority—estimating it at about 20 percent—who "attend Mass and go to Communion regularly, go to Confession occasionally, think of themselves as 'orthodox' Christians, and read the Scriptures whenever they can. They are very concerned about the poor and the vulnerable, expressing what many of them consider the very heart of Christ's gospel." Some in this group are considering priesthood or religious life, planning to marry in the church, raise their kids in it, and see themselves as the church's future.[13]

---

8. Ibid., 83.

9. William D. Dinges, "Faith, Hope and (Excessive) Individualism," in *Handing on the Faith: The Church's Mission and Challenge*, ed. Robert P. Imbelli (New York: Herder and Herder, 2006) 33.

10. Thomas P. Rausch, *Being Catholic in a Culture of Choice* (Collegeville, MN: Liturgical Press, 2006) 4–7.

11. D'Antonio, *American Catholics Today*, 143–44.

12. Rausch, *Being Catholic*, 87ff.

13. D'Antonio, *American Catholics Today*, 81.

One of the difficulties is how to identify this group. Some dismiss them as neoconservatives, traditionalists, or John Paul II Catholics. Others call them evangelical Catholics.[14]

3. The Pew Forum Survey (2008)

According to the recent Pew Forum Study, more than one-quarter (28 percent) of Americans have left the faith in which they were raised for another religious tradition. Among these traditions, Catholicism has experienced the greatest net loss in members. While nearly one in three Americans (31 percent) were raised in the Catholic faith, today fewer than one in four (24 percent) continue to identify themselves as Catholic. Approximately one-third of the survey respondents who say they were raised Catholic no longer describe themselves as Catholic.[15] This means that roughly 10 percent of all Americans are former Catholics, a percentage much higher among people in their 20s and early 30s according to John Cusick.[16]

At the same time, these statistics can be deceptive, as Mark Gray and Joseph Harris have pointed out. The Catholic Church is the largest in terms of net losses, but it is also the largest Christian community in the United States. The numbers would be even worse if the Catholic Church were losing members at the rate of the other Christian churches. Significantly, the authors note, "None of these other Christian churches has had as much success as the Catholic Church in retaining adult members who were raised in the faith."[17]

Still the lack of involvement of young Catholics in the life of the church is a matter of concern. In the view of the Woodstock Theological Center's Thomas Reese, the reason young Catholics under forty are not joining groups like Call to Action is not because they agree with the bishops. It's because they don't care. "Younger people are simply leaving the church, rather than stay and try to reform it."[18] But many young Catholics have trouble with the church precisely as an institution. They disagree with official church teaching on homosexuality and other issues of sexuality and gender.

14. William L. Portier, "Here Come the Evangelical Catholics," *Communio* 31 (Spring 2004) 35–66.

15. http://pewresearch.org/pubs/743/united-states-religion.

16. John Cusick, "Priest Calls for New Strategies to Keep Young Adults in Church," Catholic News Service, May 6, 2008, http://www.catholicnews.com/data/stories/cns/0802495 .htm.

17. Mark M. Gray and Joseph Claude Harris, "A Phantom Crisis: Are Catholics Leaving the Church in Droves? Not Really," *America* 199/2 (2008) 26.

18. Margaret Ramirez, "Catholic Activists Mark End of an Era," at www.chicagotribune .com/news/local/chi-call-to-action_ bd01jun01,0,2045666.story.

Former Catholics constitute one of the largest religious groups or "denominations" in the country. At the same time, the total number of Catholics in the United States has remained relatively stable because of Catholic immigrants, particularly Hispanics. Though Hispanics represent only 12 percent of Catholics seventy and older, they account for nearly half of all Catholics ages eighteen to twenty-nine (45 percent). English-speaking Hispanic Catholics were found to be no different from other Catholics in their commitment to the church, their identity as Catholics, or in their core beliefs, differing only in rating "the teaching authority claimed by the Vatican" and "Church involvement in activities directed toward social justice" above "the Catholic Church's teachings that oppose same-sex marriage" and "the Catholic Church's teachings that oppose abortion."[19]

4. Seeds of Hope (2008)

More encouraging is Tim Muldoon's book, *Seeds of Hope*. A theologian and assistant to the vice president for mission and identity at Boston College, his book is an insightful approach to young Catholics. The largest group among Catholics in the United States, they are both insiders and outsiders; they know some of the Catholic tradition's language and basic ideas, but what has really shaped them and their worldview is popular culture. This point is key. "Instead of standing firmly with the community of faith in order to critique U.S. culture, they stand firmly within U.S. culture in order to critique the Church."[20]

If Muldoon acknowledges what other surveys of young Catholics have pointed out, his approach is more sympathetic. He admits that in comparison with pre–Vatican II and Vatican II Catholics, they are poorly catechized, at least in terms of traditional standards. They are individualistic to the core, products of a consumerist culture in which authority has been decentralized, with "multipolar networks of authorities" available on the Internet, so that religion, spirituality, even questions of faith and morals are matters of personal choice and preference, like choosing clothing or food.[21]

Yet he argues that these young Catholics "are arguably the most sophisticated cohort when it comes to their internalization of the most radical teachings of Vatican II: on the relationship between Catholicism and other religious traditions, on the nature of religious freedom, and on the dignity

19. D'Antonio, *American Catholics Today*, 169.

20. Tim Muldoon, *Seeds of Hope: Young Adults and the Catholic Church in the United States* (New York: Paulist Press, 2008) 9.

21. Ibid., 176–77.

of the conscience."[22] They may be only nominal Catholics, may not attend church on a regular basis, may or may not believe all the teachings of the church; but "they have developed ways of looking at the world that will be enhanced, deepened through contact with those thinkers that have helped the Church to consider the implications of the gospel in the postmodern world."[23] Tom Beaudoin calls this a "performative" literacy, in contrast to a "linguistic" literacy.[24] Others, however, might argue that these are social or cultural values as much as Catholic ones.

On liturgical questions such as the role of women and extraordinary ministers of the Eucharist, these young adults are less concerned with continuity with the Church's tradition than they are "with whether the position is continuous with the world they live in."[25] Noting that liturgical symbolism is multivalent, Muldoon asks that we consider those who are left out:

> Even the most joyful liturgical celebrations have their darker sides. The celebration of communion is at the same time a manifestation of our failures at communion: with non-Catholics who might be present, with divorced and remarried Catholics, with those who consider themselves too sinful to communicate. The celebration of marriage, too, is a joyful event with a dark side, for those who are unmarried yet desiring marriage or for those recently divorced.[26]

With their sympathy to concerns of their culture, these young adults may well have something to teach the church.

5. Young Adults and Their Future in Ministry (2008)

The Lilly-funded young adult Catholics and ministry study is also encouraging. According to a preliminary report, most of the respondents said they view lay ministry as a call from God. Nearly half of the young men and more than a third of the women said they have at one time seriously considered ministry as a priest or religious. Following other career paths and a desire for marriage were most often cited as the primary reasons for not pursuing ordination.[27]

---

22. Ibid., 50.

23. Ibid., 51.

24. Tom Beaudoin, "In Praise of Young Adult Faith: Post–Vatican II Formation Produced Strong Performative Literacy," *Celebration* 33/6 (June 2004).

25. Muldoon, *Seeds of Hope*, 110; see also Kate Dugan and Jen Owens, eds., *From the Pews in the Back: Young Women and Catholicism* (Collegeville, MN: Liturgical Press, 2009).

26. Muldoon, *Seeds of Hope*, 127.

27. See "Young Adult Catholics and Their Future in Ministry," 4–5, at www.emerging models.org.

Some Initial Reflections

The results of these surveys of young American Catholics should cause us concern. We can no longer presume a commitment to the institutional church that the pre–Vatican II and even the Vatican II generation took for granted. Behind this loss of an institutional commitment lies a shift in popular consciousness from a juridical church which could compel obedience and participation to a church as a voluntary association. In a juridical church one was obligated under pain of sin to attend Mass, baptize one's children, marry before an authorized minister "in the church," and contribute to the support of the church. But as Charles Morris has observed: "After Vatican II, notions of Hell, damnation, and mortal sin, almost overnight, virtually disappeared from the American Church."[28] That fear is no longer a motivating factor for young people is hardly a negative; the church needs to win their minds and especially their hearts.

The researchers that produced *American Catholics Today* devised an index to measure church commitment, based on frequency of Mass attendance, importance of the Catholic Church in their lives, and whether they would ever consider leaving the Catholic Church. In the 2005 survey pre–Vatican II Catholics had the highest high commitment scores, 43 percent, while Vatican II Catholics scored 20 percent. Post–Vatican II Catholics declined by 7 points from the 1999 survey to 17 percent with a high commitment, while among the Millennials (born 1979–87) there was no one who scored high. "Because older Catholics have higher commitment than young adults, one cannot expect any increase in high-commitment Catholics in the near future."[29]

Thus for most young Catholics today, the church is a voluntary institution, not one that can command their loyalty. They no longer see it as one of the most important parts of their lives. Less than a quarter are involved regularly in the church's communal sacramental life, and the majority disagrees with its teaching on a number of gender, sexuality, and reproductive issues.

At the same time, a number of positive points have emerged that should be noted. First, these young Catholics are not lacking in generosity. This needs to be stressed. Many are interested in service; indeed, they think that service is intrinsic to being a Christian. They show great tolerance for those who are different, a tolerance which they do not always find in the institutional church. Robin Ryan notes that "they are less trusting of official church pronouncements, and they insist on representation for groups in the church

28. Charles R. Morris, *American Catholic* (New York: Random House, 1997) 356.
29. D'Antonio, *American Catholics Today*, 39.

whose voices have not been heard, especially women."[30] My colleague Michael Horan observes that young adults "are highly suspicious of religious superiority, or dialogue that engenders religious strife between religions groups."[31] John Cusick says that many young Catholics have problems with official teaching on marriage and women's issues and official attitudes towards gays and lesbians. They have grown up with gay and lesbian friends or coworkers, and they see the church as being antigay. They have difficulty integrating that with church teachings on loving one another.[32]

Cusick is not the only one to make this point. The "Young Adult Catholics and their Future in Ministry" report was divided on some of these questions. The researchers said in their summary:

> They are of two minds about whether the Church should go back to tradition and reject modern teaching. One faction advocates holding fast to tradition and avoiding watering down the faith, while another faction urges the Church to relate more to modern life and changing times. We cannot say which group is larger. Similarly, one faction recommends married priests and women priests while another is opposed, and one faction stresses reaching out to all people, including homosexuals, while another rejects all homosexuality.[33]

In her book *Sex and the Soul*, Donna Freitas argues that young Catholics, accustomed to pouring out their most intimate thoughts and experiences on MySpace and Facebook or in journals, are not as apathetic as they might seem to those whose research is conducted through phone calls and personal interviews. When young people are asked to write about their beliefs in private, the picture that emerges is often different, more nuanced, even passionate.[34]

Thus Robin Ryan's caution about easy generalizations should be taken seriously. These young adults often reflect the same wide-ranging diversity present in the Catholic Church in the United States today.[35] While some of those considering vocations have a more traditional spirituality and ecclesiology, others are more prophetic, and their theological instincts are often different. Sympathetic commentators like Tim Muldoon can give insight

30. Robin Ryan, "How Young Catholics See Themselves in the Church," *Horizon* (Spring 2007) 16.

31. Michael Horan, "A Bold Design Built on Rock: Constructing a Plan for Adolescent Catechesis," in *Source Book on Adolescent Catechesis*, vol. 2 (Washington, DC: NCEA, 2009) 3.

32. Cusick, "Priest Calls for New Strategies."

33. "Young Adult Catholics and Their Future in Ministry," 30.

34. Donna Freitas, *Sex and the Soul: Judging Sexuality, Spirituality, Romance, and Religion on America's College Campuses* (New York: Oxford University Press, 2008) 53–54.

35. Ryan, "How Young Catholics See Themselves," 14.

about what forms young Catholics today and how they might be engaged in the church's mission. If the church is to carry out that mission, it needs the energy, vitality, and creativity of the young.

Strategies

In an era of diminished commitment to the church, how can those involved in working with young Catholics help them become more engaged in the church's life, even to offer their own lives to the service of the church? What strategies might the church apply? This is part of a larger problem today, that of passing on the faith to the next generation. Recently, two conferences addressed this question. One was held at Boston College in September 2004. Its papers were published in a volume edited by Robert Imbelli, entitled *Handing on the Faith*.[36] The second conference met a month later at the University of Southern California, resulting in the volume edited by James Heft, *Passing on the Faith*.[37] I will draw on these studies, among other works.

If the church is to effectively reach its younger members, I would suggest stressing the following points.

1. Importance of Experience

Religious commentators like Philip Jenkins identify Pentecostalism as perhaps the most successful social movement of the past century, with the potential to surpass the one billion mark before 2050.[38] While this growth has taken place chiefly in the southern hemisphere, there is a lesson to be learned from the growth of Pentecostalism for global Christianity. In a perceptive comment, Renato Poblete, a Chilean Jesuit, attributes the effectiveness of the Pentecostals to their emphasis on a subjective experience of God, something he says has long been lost sight of in Western theology.[39] Poblete's Jesuit tradition also privileges experience. Just as Ignatius of Loyola stressed the importance of the imagination in prayer in his Spiritual Exercises, he frequently used the Spanish verbs *gustar* (to taste) and *sentir* (to experience, to perceive through the senses) to emphasize a knowledge rooted in experience. The second annotation at the beginning of the Exercises says that "it

36. Robert P. Imbelli, ed., *Handing on the Faith: The Church's Mission and Challenge* (New York: Crossroad, 2006).

37. James L. Heft, ed., *Passing on the Faith: Transforming Traditions for the Next Generation of Jews, Christians, and Muslims* (New York: Fordham University Press, 2006).

38. Philip Jenkins, *The Next Christendom: The Coming of Global Christianity* (New York: Oxford University Press, 2002) 7–8.

39. Renato Poblete, "The Catholic Church and Latin America's Pentecostals," *Origins* 27/43 (1998) 719–20.

is not abundance of knowledge that fills and satisfies the soul, but the inward sense (*sentir*) and taste (*gustar*) of things." Thus affectivity is not antithetical to critical thinking but often the path to insight and understanding.

Young adults also privilege experience over theoretical knowledge or teachings based on authority. Nothing, except perhaps a genuinely religious home, has greater impact on teenagers today than their high school *Kairos* retreats, with their powerful personal testimonies from their peers. The authors of *American Catholics Today* suggest that more effort should be put into supporting small Christian communities as well as faith-sharing and prayer groups.[40]

Many young people today are looking for some experience of community in which they can share with their peers their own personal struggles, particularly their own religious journeys. In a study of small Christian communities (SCC) conducted between 1995 and 1998, researchers found that young adults were not to be found in significant numbers among the many SCCs studied, but interestingly enough, while only 26 percent of Catholics between the ages of 19 and 39 in a national sample said they went to Mass at least weekly, 90 percent of those in campus small Christian communities said they did. While this may indicate that those students joining SCCs were the ones most likely to be weekly Mass attendees, it is still a significant fact.[41]

At my own university in Los Angeles, three of the most effective ways of getting our students in deeper touch with their faith are directed retreats and Christian Life Communities (CLCs), both sponsored by campus ministry, and cross-cultural study abroad programs, to be considered below. Each of these privilege experience. There is always a waiting list for these retreats.

The most successful retreat is a four-day "Silent Retreat" that takes place during the Christmas recess. Generally about thirty students make the retreat. Each student has a director, they are expected to spend four hours a day in prayer, and they have generally prepared for the retreat with spiritual direction, to make sure they are able to talk comfortably about their prayer experience.

We also have over fifty CLC groups on campus, faith-sharing groups of five to eight students, many of them with an adult guide. Actually these are "pre-communities," as they are not officially affiliated at the national or world level with the international CLC community.[42] Even when some of

40. D'Antonio, *American Catholics Today*, 151.

41. See William V. D'Antonio, "Appendix I: College and University Campus Communities," in Bernard J. Lee with William V. D'Antonio et al, *The Catholic Experience of Small Christian Communities* (New York: Paulist Press, 2000) 148–55.

42. See Thomas P. Rausch, "Christian Life Communities for Jesuit University Students?" *Studies in the Spirituality of Jesuits* 36/1 (Spring 2004).

the undergraduate students in these CLC groups are not regularly participating in the worship life of the campus, they provide an effective opportunity for them to talk about God, their faith, and their religious commitments with their peers in a confidential, informal setting. These small groups also offer young adults the opportunity to exercise leadership in ways that are often not available in the church. Identity is also a big issue for many undergraduates, as is evident from the fascination of so many young people with web sites like MySpace and Facebook. They are looking for experiences that will help them discover who they are, what gifts they have, and how they are possibly being called.

But important as experience is, it is not sufficient. Terrence Tilley speaks of the exhaustion of the Enlightenment emphasis on the "turn to the subject" and the "turn to experience." Referencing the works of Gustavo Gutiérrez, Roberto Goizueta, and Stanley Hauerwas, he says that the postliberal and liberationist turn to practice is even more important than experience: "The Enlightenment individual subject has been replaced by the community-shaped agent, and experience has been replaced by practice. . . . Whereas experience is something that happens to a subject, an agent engages in practice."[43] This brings up the question of mission.

2. Renewed Emphasis on Mission

Vincent Miller, in his book *Consuming Religion*, refers to the Hoge study on young adult Catholics to argue that a "generation of Catholics who are in their thirties has been socialized to see themselves as active agents of their religious beliefs, but as Catholics they have not been socialized to think of themselves as agents of their tradition."[44] Like their peers, they construct their own religious visions or spiritualities, which are essentially private. These young Catholics have no sense that they have something to hand back to their tradition from which they have drawn. They are passive consumers.

William D'Antonio and his colleagues recommend a renewed emphasis on mission as a way of increasing the next generation's attachment to the church, advice echoed by Marti Jewell of the Emerging Models of Pastoral Leadership project as well as by Muldoon.[45] If young adults place a priority

43. Terrence W. Tilley, *The Disciples' Jesus: Christology as Reconciling Practice* (Maryknoll, NY: Orbis Books, 2008) 30.

44. Vincent J. Miller, *Consuming Religion: Christian Faith and Practice in a Consumer Culture* (New York: Continuum, 2004) 212.

45. D'Antonio, *American Catholics Today*, 150; Marti R. Jewell and Dean R. Hoge, "Will They Serve? A New Survey Looks at Young People's Attitudes Toward Ministry," *America* 199/2 (2008) 19; Tim Muldoon, "Sowing the Seeds for Ministry," in the same issue, 22.

on experience, they are often generous and attracted to opportunities for service. More than half of the respondents in the Lilly-funded "Young Catholics and their Future in Ministry" said that the church needs to move faster to empower laypeople in ministry.[46]

The present emphasis on" community-based" or service learning courses in undergraduate as well as graduate education brings mission and experience together. Service learning always means some kind of experiential learning that involves service of others. It has been defined as

> a type of experiential education in which students participate in service to the community and reflect on their involvement in such a way as to gain further understanding of course content and of the discipline and its relation to social needs and an enhanced sense of civic responsibility.[47]

Programs variously identified as fieldwork, alternative spring breaks, semester- or yearlong immersion experiences in impoverished countries, whether for social justice or language, are designed to bring students into contact with the poor on a very personal level. They might involve direct service to the poor by working in soup kitchens, tutoring or teaching children, working in nursing homes or ministering to persons with AIDS, building or rehabilitating homes for the disadvantaged in programs like Habitat for Humanity, engaging in community organizing or development programs. Some young adults choose to give several years of their lives to post-college service through programs such as the Jesuit Volunteer Corps, the Holy Cross Associates, the Maryknoll Lay Missioners, and the Good Shepherd Volunteers.[48]

When I ponder how we might tailor the academic program of our university to give our students a greater sense for what we describe as our Jesuit mission, "the service of faith and the promotion of justice," nothing comes closer to the type of truly transformative educational experiences than these national or international service trips which take our students outside their own, often privileged, locations and involve them with the lives of others who are less fortunate. Some take our students to post-Katrina New Orleans, homeless advocacy in Washington DC, environmental restoration in Utah, or involvement in the struggle for farm workers' rights with the Dolores

---

46. "Young Adult Catholics and Their Future in Ministry," 20.

47. Julie A. Hatcher and Robert G. Bringle, "Bridging the Gap Between Service and Learning," *College Teaching* 45 (1997) 153, cited in *From Cloister to Commons: Concepts and Models for Service-Learning in Religious Studies*, ed. Richard Devine, Joseph A. Favazza, and F. Michael McLain (Washington, DC: American Association for Higher Education, 2002) 1.

48. See Vincent Gragnani, "The New, Lay Face of Missionaries," *America* (July 30, 2007).

Huerta Foundation. Other students go to Mexico, Central America, Latin America, the Philippines, Cambodia, or Africa. Some of our students have been on several of these trips.

For example, during spring break in 2008 one group of eleven students traveled to Quito, Ecuador, and spent the week getting to know people there assisted by *El Centro del Muchacho Trabajador* (Center for Working Boys). Another group of twelve went to San Salvador in a program coordinated by the Association of Jesuit Colleges and Universities (AJCU), centered at the UCA, the University of Central America. Joined by another large group of students from Boston College, they visited the hospital where Oscar Romero was assassinated, the site of the massacre at El Mozote in 1981, and the Jesuit residence at the UCA where the six Jesuits and two women were murdered in 1989. One of the students who went to Quito told me that he had reopened the question of a religious vocation that previously he had put on hold. He has since entered the Jesuits.

Even more effective are semester-long, cross-cultural immersion courses in similar venues. I have seen students who have been transformed by such educational experiences. Being in a completely new life situation, and more importantly, getting to know very ordinary people, poor people whose lives are so different from their own, opens their eyes and touches their hearts. A student who had spent a semester at the AJCU *Casa de la Solidaridad* program in San Salvador wrote the following:

> Upon my return from El Salvador, I began to feel as though my business major was no longer meaningful, purposeful, or life-giving for me. I began to reflect on my holistic experience and search for the deepest desires of my heart. Whenever I thought about my business major, I always thought this: I would go to work so I can make money so I can go to work. The logic of it became depressingly circular. When I was most honest with myself, I came to the clear realization that the business way of life was simply not for me.

We need to ask, how might local churches find ways to allow young people to share experientially in the church's mission? With some creativity, there are many opportunities to involve them in works of evangelization, ministry, and direct service to the disadvantaged which could help them experience a church not of rules and rituals but of service. Young adults should be invited to serve on parish and diocesan pastoral councils. Offering them ways to become involved in the church's mission is one way of extending to them a welcome that they do not always feel when they come to church. One told me, "I feel more welcome in a mall than in a church. When you enter the GAP or some store, you are immediately asked, what are you looking for, how can I help?"

3. A Welcoming Liturgy

Catholicism is an essentially ecclesial tradition; it places a high value on ritual, particularly the Eucharist, the liturgical celebration at the center of our life of faith. Yet less than a fourth of young adult Catholics regular attend Sunday Mass. It is not, I suspect, that young Catholics are necessarily against ritual expressions of their faith. Some find the Mass too ritualistic; they are not challenged by the homilies or invited to become actively involved, in spite of the multiplication of liturgical ministries today. Furthermore, their absence does not necessarily mean a lack of interest in the church.[49] How can we better invite young adults into our liturgical prayer in the way that the brothers of Taizé invite thousands of young people on pilgrimage to their monastic community in Burgundy into their prayer?

As noted earlier, Muldoon argues that for many young people church membership and liturgy makes sense "only to the extent that it sheds light on the rest of the world they live in."[50] This is what Latina/o theologians refer to as *lo cotidiano*, the ordinary and everyday. Since many young people have not grown up "at home" in the church, they must be made to feel welcome. This is not a question of revising the liturgy but of finding ways to manifest that young people are welcome. "The new challenge, the challenge for the postmodern era, is that the liturgy be a mystagogy of communion."[51]

Muldoon makes some concrete suggestions: Is the liturgical community diverse, ethnically, socioeconomically, generationally? Does the liturgy make them welcome, in its greetings, ushering, welcoming even those who are late or "improperly" dressed, as young adults often have a different sense of propriety? Do its symbols respond to popular culture, so that it addresses the world they live in? Is its language inclusive? Is it focused only on family life, or does it address specifically that large population of single people, many of whom are discerning the single life as a vocation? How does it welcome new members, by explaining the parish envelope system, or by inquiring about their interests or needs? One very successful parish in Los

---

49. See Tim Muldoon, "Sowing the Seeds for Ministry," *America* 199/2 (2008) 25; also Alice Kearney Alwin, "Christ and the Cooks; Ministry Beyond the Liturgy for Young Adults," ibid., 32.

50. Muldoon, *Seeds of Hope*, 110. John Cusick says something similar; he calls for a "new apologetics" for young adults and "satellite sites" away from the parish where they can gather ("Priest Calls for New Strategies").

51. Muldoon, *Seeds of Hope*, 113.

Angeles, known as a "welcome back parish," greets new members at a "welcome table," asks them about their interests, and contacts those who leave their names and phone numbers *within the next week*.[52]

Some students are attracted to other ritual expressions of their faith. On our campus Taizé Prayer, particularly Prayer around the Cross, and eucharistic adoration both attract a regular group of undergraduates. Both are experiences of prayer that combine ritual with a participation that gets the students out of the pews and allows them more active participation. Taizé especially places a high value on silence. Those present join in the chant, sit on the floor or prostrate; many will come forward to kiss or lay their heads on the cross. Young people at Taizé are moved, not by something designed for them, "but by a brief participation in a practice, a way of life, engaged in 365 days a year by the hundred resident monks."[53]

Eucharistic adoration is also making a comeback on many of our campuses. On our campus it combines Catholic adoration of the Blessed Sacrament with a more evangelical "praise and worship" style of prayer—contemporary praise songs and a student reflection or meditation. Furthermore, such services allow the students to take leadership roles closed to them in more traditional church services. Lamenting the loss of the rich devotional life of the Catholic Church after the Second Vatican Council, Vincent Miller observes that "devotions provided a much more active set of practices for the laity to engage in during the liturgy."[54]

4. A Willingness to Challenge Young People

Some of my students who are more involved in living their faith and trying to find their place in the church say that we need to challenge them more. Too often, campus ministry programs, homilies at campus liturgies, and faculty and staff seem reluctant to challenge young people. There is a tendency to make everything "nice," to dumb down the challenge of the Gospel and of Christian discipleship. Some of our students are there because it's the place to be, to see and be seen. Others want to be touched, challenged, given a new vision, changed.

In the consumer culture of our contemporary world, many are looking for stability, truth, meaning, for something to give their lives to. Imagine if we asked our young adults to give two years of their lives to church work

---

52. Ibid., 117–27; see Thomas P. Rausch, "Evangelization and Liturgy," in *Evangelizing America*, ed. Rausch (New York: Paulist Press, 2004) 79.

53. Jack Miles, "The Leisure of Worship and the Worship of Leisure," in Heft, *Passing on the Faith*, 258–59.

54. Miller, *Consuming Religion*, 217.

or social justice through volunteer programs such as the Mormons do. We need to make them familiar with the universal call to holiness which is stressed by Vatican II (LG, chap. 5) and implied by their baptism. They are called to become saints.

Conclusion

The purpose of my reflections here is intended to be more diagnostic than judgmental, to give some impressions based on my own impressions after years of teaching and from a familiarity with recent writing on young Catholics. Let me try to draw some summary conclusions.

At the June 2008 meeting of the Catholic Theological Society of America, in a session devoted to "Handing on the Faith," Tim Muldoon surprised those present by calling for a recovery of "a measure of traditionalism," especially in regard to our formation of young Catholics. Specifically, he expressed a wish to see more priests and nuns in habits, called for making room for rote memorization as a moment in a larger dynamic, and said that Catholic colleges and universities need to be more "old fashioned." Muldoon is hardly a traditionalist!

What he is suggesting are strategies to address what is often called the religious illiteracy of so many young Catholics. Or perhaps more politely put, the fact that they often lack familiarity with the stories and root metaphors of the Catholic tradition and with its vocabulary and grammar. Thus I am less sanguine than William D'Antonio, James Davidson, and Andrew Greeley about young Catholics maintaining their Catholic identity, adhering to the "core doctrines" of the faith,[55] in spite of their diminishing institutional commitment and lack of familiarity with the language and stories of the tradition.

Referring to Charles Taylor's view that inarticulacy undermines the possibilities of reality, Christian Smith argues that "religious faith, practice, and commitment can be no more than indistinctly real when people cannot talk much about them. Articulacy fosters reality."[56] Similarly, for Robert Wilken, language defines who we are. He writes that the faith is handed on embedded in language. It is not a set of abstract beliefs but a world of shared associations and allusions. Christian speech is not primarily the technical vocabulary

55. D'Antonio, *American Catholics Today*, 34–35; Andrew Greeley, *The Catholic Revolution: New Wine, Old Wineskins, and the Second Vatican Council* (Berkeley: University of California Press, 2004) 110–13.

56. Christian Smith, "Moral Therapeutic Deism," in Heft, *Passing on the Faith*, 70; his reference is to Charles Taylor, *Sources of the Self* (Cambridge: Harvard University Press, 1989), and "Self-Interpreting Animals," in *Human Agency and Language* (Cambridge: Cambridge University Press, 1985) 45–76.

of Christian doctrine. "It is the language of the psalms, the stories of the patriarchs, the parables of the Gospels, the moral vocabulary of Paul's Epistles."[57] Such a sense for the faith is not cultivated simply by learning the *Catechism of the Catholic Church.*

I think Hoge, who argues that young adult Catholics like being Catholic in subjective terms, but are all but indistinguishable from mainline Protestants, is more insightful here.[58] He says that significant numbers of young Catholics no longer see the Catholic Church as unique, the pope as necessary, the church's structure as important, or tradition as a source of objective truth.[59] They like the church's commitment to social justice but for the most part are unfamiliar with its social doctrine. "If the relationship between social justice and a specifically Catholic identity were more immediate to young adult Catholics, their perspective might be more concerned with structural approaches, aggregate effects, power, and institutional systems—in keeping with contemporary church teaching regarding social justice." They think that being religious means being a good person, approaching social problems with acts of charity.[60] William Dinges characterizes tradition for this group as "not so much a binding community of discipleship and obligation as a toolkit of sacred wares for constructing a personal spiritual identity."[61]

Most of the surveys we have considered point out that young Catholics have difficulties with the official church's teaching on gender, sexual issues, divorce and remarriage, and particularly the role of women and homosexuality. The D'Antonio survey reports that none of the Millennials scored high on commitment to the church.[62] It also emphasized that "young adults—more than older Catholics—are faced with participating in an institution that does not reflect their worldview. The Church is also confronted with ministering to young adults who disagree with many of its policies and practices."[63] When the church is perceived by so many young adults as a voluntary institution to which one chooses to belong, the growing divide between official church teaching and what young adult Catholics believe becomes an issue that the church needs to address. The church also needs to find more effec-

57. Robert Louis Wilken, "The Church's Way of Speaking," in Imbelli, *Handing on the Faith,* 95.

58. Dean R. Hoge, et al, *Young Adult Catholics: Religion in the Culture of Choice* (Notre Dame, IN: University of Notre Dame Press, 2001) 223.

59. Ibid., 221.

60. Ibid., 224.

61. Dinges, "Faith, Hope and (Excessive) Individualism," 37.

62. D'Antonio, *American Catholics Today*, 39.

63. Ibid., 82.

tive ways to tap into the generosity of young people, to challenge them to serve and become involved more directly in the church's mission.

In the following chapters we will consider some current efforts to expand the walls of our classrooms and the experience of our students, bringing them into conversation with a wider world and, hopefully, touching their hearts.

Chapter 5

Catholic Studies

Don J. Briel

The phenomenon of Catholic Studies cannot adequately be understood without a prior consideration of certain fundamental tensions that mark modern higher education as a whole. These broader tensions characterize Catholic universities in specific and important ways. One may hesitate to affirm Lammenais' judgment that Napoleon's creation of the modern French university was the most pernicious act of his reign, but Lammenais himself had no hesitation in insisting that Napoleon "raised this monstrous edifice as a monument of his hatred for future generations; it was as though he wanted to rob the human race even of hope."[1]

Nonetheless, in recent years many well-known academics and cultural critics have begun to question both the coherence and the relevance of the contemporary university. Several years ago, in a widely publicized lecture delivered at Georgetown and later in a paper delivered before a meeting of Catholic scholars in Chicago, Cardinal Francis George insisted that a university without a unifying vision is merely a high-class trade school, and he argued that many of the most important institutions of higher learning in the United States had moved far in this direction.[2] In his account of the decline of American undergraduate education, the former dean of Harvard College, Harry Lewis, agreed with this general assessment in arguing that although it is true that "old institutional structures survive," nonetheless, "many have

---

1. Cited in Michael Burleigh, *Earthly Powers: The Clash of Religion and Politics in Europe from the French Revolution to the Great War* (New York: HarperCollins, 2005) 133.

2. Francis Cardinal George, "The Catholic Mission Today in Higher Education," paper presented at Georgetown University, October 1997; and "Universities that Are Truly Catholic and Truly Academic," paper presented at the Inaugural Convocation of Presidents and Faculty Members of Chicago are a Catholic Colleges and Universities, September 1998.

lost their meaning. The curriculum is richer than ever, but it is no longer wrapped around any identifiable ideals."[3]

Similarly, C. John Sommerville has argued that the modern university's resolute commitment to an ideological secularism, one which reduces the perennial human questions of meaning and ultimate concern to arbitrary private values, has produced a crisis not only of confidence but also of co-herence. "If our universities are to become more than professional schools," Sommerville argues,

> then rationalism needs to be in dialogue with other "traditions of inquiry." For the most important matters in life include such matters as hope, depres-sion, trust, purpose, and wisdom. If secularism purges such concerns from the curriculum for lack of a way to address them, the public may conclude that the football team really is the most important part of the university. But if they are taken up, we will find ourselves using terms that seem to belong in a religious discourse. We have dodged this issue by saying that true, good, just are all political, meaning that they can't be discussed but only voted on. But in fact they could be discussed, if our discussions were to recognize a dimension of ultimacy.[4]

Several decades earlier Christopher Dawson had described the basic frame-work of modern culture as "unitary," for in such a culture, he argued,

> there is little room for the concepts which are fundamental to the Catholic or Christian view—the supernatural, spiritual authority, God and the soul—in fact, the whole notion of the transcendent. So unless students can learn something of Christian culture as a whole—the world of Christian thought and the Christian way of life and the norms of the Christian com-munity—they are placed in a position of cultural estrangement—the social inferiority of the ghetto without its old self-containedness and self-sufficiency.[5]

And so it was necessary, Dawson insisted, that students have an integrated and comprehensive sense of Christian culture as a whole so that the Christian way of life could be seen "not as a number of isolated precepts imposed by ecclesiastical authority, but as a cosmos of spiritual relations embracing heaven and earth and uniting the order of social and moral life with the order

---

3. Harry R. Lewis, *Excellence without a Soul: How a Great University Forgot Education* (New York: Public Affairs, 2006) xii.

4. C. John Sommerville, *The Decline of the Secular University* (New York: Oxford Uni-versity Press, 2006) 22.

5. Christopher Dawson, *The Crisis of Western Education* (New York: Sheed and Ward, 1961) 146–47.

of divine grace."[6] But both modern culture and the modern university are far more modest in their commitments. As Lewis noted:

> The university has lost, indeed has willingly surrendered, its moral authority to shape the souls of its students. Harvard wants students to be safe and to be healthy, but security and therapy are the limits of its ambitions. Harvard articulates no ideal of what it means to be a good person, as opposed to a well person.[7]

Clearly, to the degree that this is true, Harvard is far from unique in this shift to a more therapeutic approach to student life and formation.

Catholic Studies Programs

We do well to escape the intellectual ghettos of the past, but we should be more attentive to the new ghettos we often erect to replace them, and it is in this connection that I would like now to turn to the development of Catholic Studies programs at American Catholic universities. It is sometimes argued that Catholic Studies marks a return to the ghetto of Catholic isolationism, but I suspect that Dawson was ultimately right in arguing that many of the self-imposed ghettos of the contemporary academy pose a more dangerous isolation from the deepest human longings: for the transcendent, for spiritual authority, for God. It is surely the case that both the curricula and the animating vision of Catholic Studies programs vary widely. Some may well focus rather narrowly on a cultural studies model, but I suspect all of them to a greater or lesser degree developed out of a concern to recover this more integrated understanding of Catholic thought and culture that has in large measure been obscured in recent history.

Some have argued that the new emphasis on Catholic Studies within Catholic universities simply confirms the fundamental loss of a coherent Catholic identity for the university as a whole. However, I am not persuaded that this is the case. It had always been true that only a relatively small minority of faculty at Catholic institutions systematically engaged the complex intellectual search for a unity of knowledge arising out of a Catholic vision of reality. In the past this task was largely exercised by the religious communities that founded and sustained these institutions, communities whose own wide-ranging interdisciplinary conversations established a framework and context for the university as a whole. We have not yet fully realized the larger implications of the decline in numbers and influence of these religious com-

6. Dawson, *Crisis,* 150.
7. Lewis, *Excellence,* 159–60.

munities, the loss of which has left a significant vacuum within Catholic higher education. It is perhaps inevitable that a now more voluntary and diverse community, largely composed of lay scholars committed to an ongoing interdisciplinary reflection on the integrity of Catholic life and thought, would continue to be a minority within the larger faculty of the university.

Of course, these religious communities also held an administrative responsibility for the life of the university and so exercised authority over hiring and curriculum, but the fact remains that it has never been the case that the modern university as a whole had taken up this integrating task in a systematic way. If we hope to recover and renew this emphasis, we will need to create new institutional structures, forums for sustained conversation, new curricula, and to develop an institutional willingness to hire faculty who have specific commitment and competence for this kind of broad, interdisciplinary reflection. I think that Catholic Studies reflects one significant approach to this larger goal.

Catholic Studies initiatives are essential to this renewal of Catholic higher education, I think, but before I turn to the positive value of Catholic Studies programs for the vitality of Catholic intellectual life, let me list several things that Catholic Studies programs are not:

1. Catholic Studies programs are a necessary but insufficient response to the demands for the renewal of Catholic higher education.
2. Catholic Studies programs cannot substitute for strong programs in theology and philosophy. In fact, Catholic Studies programs both presuppose and depend upon the strength of these disciplines.
3. Catholic Studies programs do not imply a rejection of the importance of the study of other Christian traditions and other religions. Again, they assume the value of such studies.

From the point of view of the positive dimension of Catholic Studies for contemporary Catholic universities, I would stress the following contributions. Catholic higher education as a whole depends upon the creation of such programs that might remind the university of the comprehensiveness and integrity of the Catholic intellectual tradition at a time in which there is a tendency to view Catholic life and thought as a series of disconnected and arbitrary assertions and moral claims. It is in this sense that Pope John Paul II spoke of the necessity within the university to "work towards a higher synthesis of knowledge, in which alone lies the possibility of satisfying that thirst for truth which is profoundly inscribed on the heart of the human person."[8] In order for this work to be achieved, he argued, there must be

8. John Paul II, *Ex corde ecclesiae* (Washington, DC: United States Conference of Catholic Bishops, 2000) 15.

sustained attention to "interdisciplinary studies, assisted by a careful and thorough study of philosophy and theology" in order to "enable students to acquire an organic vision of reality and to develop a continuing desire for intellectual progress."[9] John Henry Newman insisted that the university could not be content to become a mere caravanserai of ideas without any organizing principle, but rather would be required to assign to each study its "own proper place and own just boundaries."[10] But the fact remains that there are few forums on our campuses for these interdisciplinary reflections on Catholic thought and culture. Without them it is inconceivable that sustained conversations of this kind could take place.

Catholic Studies programs can recover for students and faculty alike the integrity of the life of thought and prayer, of human and divine knowledge, and help to overcome the cultural and intellectual divides that separate faculty and academic departments from the work of campus ministry programs and service to the community and the church. They also provide important reminders that the vital mission of Catholic higher education is not merely imposed by ecclesiastical mandate but arises out of a deep, comprehensive, and venerable Catholic humanist tradition. This distinctive tradition of Christian humanism was expressed with characteristic eloquence by Newman in an 1856 sermon in the University Church in Dublin in which he insisted that the task of the church in relation to the university is to

> reunite things which were in the beginning joined together by God and have been put asunder by man. Some persons will say that I am thinking of confining, distorting, and stunting the growth of the intellect by ecclesiastical supervision. I have no such thought. Nor have I any thought of a compromise, as if religion must give up something, and science something. I wish the intellect to range with the utmost freedom and religion to enjoy an equal freedom; but what I am stipulating for is that they should be found in one and the same place and exemplified in the same persons. I want to destroy that diversity of centers, which puts everything into confusion by creating a contrariety of influences. I wish the same spots and the same individuals to be at once oracles of philosophy and shrines of devotion. It will not satisfy me if religion is here and science is there, and young men converse with science all day and lodge with religion in the evening. . . . I want the same roof to contain both the intellectual and the moral disci-

---

9. Ibid., 9.

10. John Henry Newman, "Christianity and Scientific Investigation," in *The Idea of a University*, ed. Martin Svaglic (Notre Dame, IN: University of Notre Dame Press, 1982) 344.

pline. . . . I want the intellectual layman to be religious and the devout ecclesiastic to be intellectual.[11]

Intellectual Integration

The inevitable complexity of university programs and audiences that now marks contemporary higher education makes it increasingly unlikely, perhaps as some have argued, unthinkable, that the integration of the university and the college that Newman had proposed, the integration of ideas and the integrity of intellectual and moral formation of students, can be pursued systematically and organically by the faculty of the university as a whole. But as I argued earlier, the systematic exploration of these issues has never been seen to be a general expectation for faculty in the modern Catholic university. The larger integration was both promoted and modeled by the founding religious order, which was able to sustain a complex sense of a large integrity to which the personal efforts and scholarly commitments of other faculty, both Catholic and non-Catholic, contributed. I am persuaded that even a major implementation of new hiring-for-mission policies, which succeeded in bringing to Catholic campuses a much larger number of faculty committed to a distinctive Catholic identity and mission, would not resolve this pressing need for integration. This task must be engaged by a relatively small number of faculty for whom this would be the principal scholarly commitment and teaching expectation. To achieve this goal it will be necessary to move beyond an academic program to a more comprehensive and complex academic center that would provide forums for interdisciplinary conversations and scholarly projects focusing on the integration of knowledge and the ultimate complementarity of faith and reason in Catholic thought.

This leads me once again to a consideration of the role of Catholic Studies. In recent years there have been a number of typologies proposed by which to differentiate various approaches taken by emerging Catholic Studies programs. These types or models have never struck me as particularly useful, since few of the programs fail to reflect many aspects of each of the various models proposed. Each of Mary Ann Hinsdale's four models, for example, is reflected in the work of Catholic Studies at the University of St. Thomas in what we see to be their genuine tension and complementarity.[12] It may be true that in the case of a campus in which a chair in Catholic Studies is devoted to the particular research interests of an individual scholar that one

11. John Henry Newman, "Intellect, the Instrument of Religious Training," in *Sermons Preached on Various Occasions* (London: Longmans, Green and Co., 1921) 13.
12. Mary Ann Hinsdale, "Catholic Studies: Models and Motives," paper presented at the conference of the American Academy of Religion, Boston, November 1999.

of these models is selectively emphasized, but I know of no successful program in the country that could be adequately described in terms of one of these models. Inevitably, Catholic Studies must engage the variety of cultures in which the Catholic Church has sought to express its deepest convictions and by which it has been shaped in that expression, and so some aspect of a cultural studies approach is to be assumed. But that concern would not preclude a close consideration of the specific claims of the complex and comprehensive intellectual tradition of the faith. In fact, it presupposes it. Such a consideration could conceivably be undertaken without any apologetic aim, but such a study would be of little interest to the students seeking a deeper sense of the unity of knowledge and an understanding of the relation of faith and reason to be found in Catholicism. And finally, issues of formation, not only in our program but in most others, have been taken up in response both to student demand and to a recognized need to recover what the Land O'Lakes Statement (see chap. 1, pg. 1) referred to as the obligation to ensure the full human and spiritual development of the student.

A Community of Scholars

One sometimes has the impression that Catholic Studies programs have been the product of authority, whether ecclesiastical or academic. Although the support of St. Thomas' president and senior administrators was critical, the impetus for the country's first Catholic Studies program was entirely that of faculty. In preparation for a national conference on the prospects for Catholic colleges and universities in the twenty-first century, a group of faculty on our campus developed a proposal for a five-year series of lectures and summer seminars exploring future challenges and opportunities for Catholic higher education. The seminars, which began in the summer of 1994, were led by external facilitators and were connected to a series of semiannual lectures in which a wide variety of Catholic and non-Catholic speakers explored the general idea of a Catholic university, the role of faculty, issues of a distinctive curriculum, academic freedom, and the role of the Catholic university in American culture. The series involved a large number of the faculty in an exploration of the mission and identity of the Catholic university and a consideration of its implications for their own teaching and scholarship in particular disciplines.

The conversations continued to be both wide ranging and vital and were in large measure made possible by a new kind of university forum provided by Catholic Studies that had begun to draw into being a community of scholars committed to extending this great conversation. Both in preparation for the seminars, and later in the course of them, a number of faculty began to focus on existing obstacles to the achievement of a distinctive Catholic identity on our campus. Acknowledging a consistent Catholic emphasis on the unity of knowledge and the ultimate complementarity of faith and reason and equally aware of John Paul II's insistence on the fact that a Catholic university was paradoxically committed to both an ongoing reflection on the truth it has received in the *Logos* and an open search for truth, we recognized that these fundamental claims were rarely explicit in the intellectual life of our campus. At the same time we realized that we had considerable strengths on which to build. As a diocesan university we had retained a sense of ecclesial identity and had, as a result, consistently sought to articulate our self-understanding in explicitly Catholic terms rather than in that of the charism of a founding religious community. We had retained strong and coherent departments of theology and philosophy with unusually large general requirements (twelve credits in theology, eight in philosophy). We had a president who was committed to and articulate about our Catholic identity and had on campus both a college and a major seminary. In addition, the university had vibrant professional and preprofessional programs that had sustained connections with the university's commitment to liberal learning and Catholic mission.

At the same time we were aware that we confronted a number of challenges in attempting to renew our Catholic identity, including the fragmentation of knowledge, in one sense an inevitable result of the proliferation of information in modern culture; the decline in religious literacy among students; the increasing specialization of disciplinary claims and of faculty training; hiring and promotion structures which rewarded that specialization and increasingly deemphasized the value of general knowledge and interdisciplinary studies; the increasing privatization of faith in modern culture and the dissociation of sensibility between the hard sciences and what were increasingly seen to be mere emotive religious claims; and the standardization of university life, partly reflecting an instrumentalization of the university itself and partly the recognition that students increasingly tended to view their university studies merely in terms of career preparation.

An Interdisciplinary Approach

These conversations eventually led to a proposal to create a new interdisciplinary program that would allow interested students to explore more systematically the complex intellectual tradition of the Catholic faith and to consider its expression within a variety of historical periods and cultural contexts. Drawing upon the strengths of faculty from a range of departments, including theology, philosophy, English, history, psychology, the natural sciences, and business, we eventually proposed both a major and minor in Catholic Studies to the faculty senate in the fall of 1992 and offered our first courses in the fall of 1993. Initial core courses included the Catholic Vision, Faith and Doubt, Literature from a Catholic Perspective, the Catholic Literary Tradition, Medieval to Modern, and Catholic Social Thought. In addition, students were required to take two courses focusing on history and the fine arts. We also created a series of team-taught courses focusing on the relation of Catholic thought to the professions of management, education, law, medicine, and engineering, and developed two Templeton award-winning courses which examined the relation of Catholic thought and the natural sciences.

The interdisciplinary character of the program was emphasized from the beginning, in the selection of faculty, the vast majority of whom had graduate degrees in more than one discipline as well as an established scholarly commitment to explore the complex interdisciplinary tradition of Catholic thought and culture; in the faculty development seminars which we created to provide consistent opportunities for interdisciplinary conversation and curricular planning; in sponsoring guest lectures and team-taught teaching opportunities; and in stipends for interdisciplinary research projects and course development. The courses were interdisciplinary in a deeper sense as well; that is, they sought not only to clarify the multiplicity of disciplines within which one might investigate the claims of Catholic thought and culture but also to integrate those perspectives and claims. In the beginning a number of these courses were cross listed with other programs. There were, of course, practical reasons for doing so. However, as numbers of majors and minors grew, it became clear that we needed to emphasize even more fully the pursuit of integration of disciplinary perspectives and this led to a revision of the core requirements for the major. The requirements now include four core courses (four-credit system):

1. CATH 101 The Search for Happiness
2. CATH 201 Paths and Practices of Catholic Spirituality
3. CATH 301 The Catholic Vision
4. CATH 401 The Church and Culture: Social Dimensions of Catholicism

In addition, students must complete twelve credits in approved philosophically, aesthetically, or historically based courses and eight credits in other approved electives.

Although we focused on the minor field, assuming that the relatively large number of university general education requirements would discourage students from pursuing the major, we did develop a major field with an expectation for a double major in a second field of study. In the spring of 1995 we graduated 2 majors and 1 minor. In the spring of 2008, 74 students graduated in Catholic Studies with double majors in over 25 fields of study; 16 of those students had attained summa cum laude honors. In the spring of 2009, 72 students graduated in Catholic Studies, including 56 majors and 16 minors, 5 of whom are triple majors. The rapid growth in the program initially surprised us, but we soon came to recognize that we were encountering a new generation of students interested in exploring the contemporary relevance of Catholic thought and culture with remarkable openness and enthusiasm. This desire for a deeper exploration of Catholic thought led to a strong preference for the major. From the beginning of the program more than 80 percent of our students have chosen the major rather than the minor field concentration.

The development of the Catholic Studies program on our campus inevitably raised a number of concerns. Would the interdisciplinary program not inevitably tend to diminish the distinctive roles of theology and philosophy in the general curriculum and in the life of the university at large? Would Catholic Studies not tend to marginalize the presence of Catholic thought on campus and thus absolve the university as a whole of its obligation to express its Catholic identity in all of its disciplines and programs? In fact, did we not run the risk of repeating the nineteenth-century pattern of marginalizing the study of religion to intellectually and geographically isolated schools of divinity? In contrast, we argued that the interdisciplinary study of Catholicism on campus would enhance rather than undermine the roles of theology and philosophy and that Catholic Studies would in this sense act as a catalyst for the renewal of Catholic life and thought on our campus.

Of course, from the beginning the Catholic Studies project at St. Thomas focused on an engagement with the university as a whole in its emphasis on the double major, on courses linking Catholic thought to specific disciplines and professions, as well as its continuing commitment to faculty development and to university-wide lectures and programs. We not only continued but expanded our faculty summer seminars with a new series focusing on particular topics ranging from the relations of science and theology, the Catholic novel, the church and baroque art in Rome, management education in a Catholic university, and the church's relations to the Third Reich. In addition, with the support of a number of deans, we developed a series of seminars on the Catholic intellectual tradition for faculty in specific schools and colleges of the university.

The Center for Catholic Studies

In the spring of 1996 the university created the Center for Catholic Studies in order to coordinate the work of the interdisciplinary program, various lecture series, and faculty development seminars, and to develop new initiatives designed to enhance opportunities for the interdisciplinary study of Catholicism on campus. That same year the first of the center's two research institutes, the John A. Ryan Institute for Catholic Social Thought, focusing on the relationship between the Catholic social tradition and business theory and practice, was created. The university has long had both vibrant undergraduate programs in business and one of the country's largest master of business administration (MBA) programs. It was within this context that the institute developed four major priorities for its work:

1. Research: The institute sponsors seminars, conferences, and publications including international conferences and seminars in the United States, Mexico, India, Belgium, Spain, and the Vatican. Many of these conferences have been cosponsored by the Pontifical Council for Justice and Peace and the International Association of Jesuit Business Schools. The institute has published eight books and dozens of articles on the relationship between Catholic social thought and business.

2. Faculty Development: The institute has worked with the dean of the college of business to create the Mission Driven Business Education Seminar based on the model of the Aspen great books seminars. It developed a series of faculty dinner conversations and seminars on special topics primarily for business faculty.

3. Curriculum Development: The institute developed a series of undergraduate team-taught courses on Christian faith and the professions. One of these courses focuses on management education and received the National Outstanding Course Award from the United States Association for Small Business and Entrepreneurship in 2002. In addition, the institute also contributed to the development of the business ethics requirement and the Reflective Manager course for the evening MBA program. The institute coordinated a conference at Notre Dame in June 2008 on business education at the Catholic university.

4. Outreach to Practitioners: The institute developed the Faith and Work Breakfast Series at St. Olaf, an urban parish in Minneapolis, in which a number of local and national speakers have reflected upon the relation of faith and work in American culture. The series is now in its thirteenth year with over one hundred participants for each of the six sessions each year. The institute also worked to implement the Seeing Things Whole Project with its focus seminars, roundtables, and retreats.

In collaboration with the Archdiocese of St. Paul and Minneapolis, we developed a number of workshops and seminars on Catholic identity and the role of Catholic social thought for Catholic high school teachers. These programs continued for several years and involved faculty from schools throughout the archdiocese. In addition, the institute worked with high school faculty on new courses incorporating Catholic social thought into the curriculum.

As well, at the request of the archdiocese, the center developed Enrichment in Catholicism, a series of lectures and discussions on the implications of the Second Vatican Council for lay ministry. In 1997, in order to provide a national forum for the interdisciplinary study of Catholicism and culture, the center launched its interdisciplinary quarterly, *Logos: A Journal of Catholic Thought and Culture*. The journal is now available in both print and online versions.

In 1998 Catholic Studies announced an affiliated program with the Dominican pontifical university, the Angelicum, which allows Catholic Studies students to spend a semester or year of study in Rome. In 1999 the university acquired a 20,000-square-foot residence on the Tiber to house students, Catholic Studies faculty, and the residence directors. The program allows our students to pursue studies at the Angelicum with others from diverse geographical and cultural backgrounds, to deepen their appreciation of the global reality of Catholicism, and to enrich their sense of Catholicism's pursuit of beauty in art, liturgy, and architecture in Rome. The program offers an integrated academic and spiritual formation with a commitment to service in the city, most frequently with the Sant'Egidio Movement or the Missionaries of Charity. There is a chaplain for the program, which also sponsors retreats, program study tours and on-site learning opportunities in the city. In senior exit interviews students have consistently emphasized the transforming power of this experience of living in an intentional community of friendship and shared faith, of exploring the comprehensive tradition of Catholic thought in a rich interdisciplinary, multicultural context, of the power of living with faculty and their families and learning of their distinct Christian vocation, of witnessing the church's service to the poor and the needy both in established religious orders and in new ecclesial movements, of the new recognition of the complex history and pervasive presence of Catholicism in Rome.

In 2000 we developed the master's program in Catholic Studies, the only graduate program of its kind in the country. The following year we announced a joint degree with the School of Law. We found quickly that the graduate program tended to draw three distinct but complementary audiences. First, there were a significant number of traditional-aged recent graduates who sought a deep interdisciplinary foundation in Catholic thought before going on to doctoral studies in a particular discipline or to professional studies in medicine, law, education, or business. Second, there were a considerable number of midcareer professionals who, having a deep sense of the imbalance of their specialized professional training and their very basic intellectual formation in faith, were drawn to an academic study of Catholicism. Finally, we found that a number of teachers, administrators, and lay ministers were eager to pursue such an interdisciplinary study of Catholicism rather than more focused courses in ministry formation. The program now enrolls ninety students from around the country and has attracted international students from Japan, China, the Philippines, and Romania. We are now exploring a variety of distance-learning opportunities.

We had begun to realize that the increasingly complex programs of Catholic Studies could not be sustained without new institutional structures to support them. It had become apparent, for example, that the academic program could not continue to develop and expand if faculty were able to pursue their interdisciplinary teaching and research only when released from their primary teaching and research obligations within a specific discipline. This led us to seek a change from the status of a program to that of a department, a change that was approved in 2001. There is now a core faculty whose principal work in the university is within Catholic Studies. In addition, however, there are primary, secondary, and adjunct appointments in Catholic Studies, which allow a number of faculty to continue to teach in Catholic Studies as well as in another department. That same year we launched our semiannual magazine, *Perspectives*, which provides an overview of the activities of all of the center's programs.

Contributions Campus-Wide

In 2002 the center coordinated the university's application to the Lilly Endowment to support "From Career to Calling," a program to promote the theological exploration of vocation. Although we created a wide number of programs across the campus, Lilly funding enabled the center to move forward with a number of its own new initiatives designed to promote vocational discernment. Included among them were an expansion of the faith and professions courses; grants for new course development and research projects; a new Latino leadership program; the Leadership Interns Program, which identifies talented junior and senior students already in leadership positions on campus and provides more intensive leadership formation for the church and civil society; the Aquinas Fellows Program, which honors undergraduate students of unusual distinction in each of the three areas of vocational discernment identified by the Lilly Endowment; residential living communities for men and women and designated floors in residence halls; service learning and retreat opportunities; internships and opportunities to learn about men's and women's religious communities, lay vocations, and diocesan priesthood. Students have organized a variety of clubs including Catholic Witness, which hosts a number of social and religious activities and collaborates with other Christian groups on campus in joint programs. In addition, Catholic Studies undergraduates developed a student club, *Caritas,* which sponsors a variety of service opportunities on and off campus, most notably a service program at Cristo Rey High School in Minneapolis.

That same year we began the renovation of Sitzmann Hall in order to accommodate the expansion of the center's programs. With a major gift from the Sitzmann family we were able to complete the renovation in January of 2003 and move into the building now containing fourteen offices, a chapel, classroom, student common room, computer lab, conference and meeting rooms, and full kitchen. This year we announced plans for an addition that will double the size of our current space in order to accommodate all of the center's programs. We broke ground for that addition in spring 2009. With the expansion we will add a larger chapel, a new classroom, offices, a graduate student center, and an elevator which will, for the first time, make the building fully accessible.

In 2005 we announced the creation of the Terrence J. Murphy Institute for Catholic Thought, Law and Public Policy, a joint venture of the Center for Catholic Studies and the School of Law. The institute's activities focus on four areas: developing curricular resources for Catholic law schools, facilitating research and scholarly discussions concerning law and the Catholic intellectual tradition, engaging and serving the community through public events, and nonpartisan public policy analysis rooted in the Catholic tradition. The institute has sponsored a number of local and national symposia in order to fulfill this larger mission. That same year we developed a new program on the Catholic-Orthodox dialogue, bringing to campus a range of speakers and cultural events to highlight the importance of mutual understanding between Eastern and Western churches. In 2007 we developed two new lecture/seminar series, the first focusing on the church and the biomedical revolution, the second on the importance of Hispanic culture for the church in the United States.

Institute for Catholic Leadership

In recent years many of the center's principal programs have been developed with the support of funding from the Lilly Endowment's program on the theological exploration of vocation. We had committed to sustaining the most successful of these programs and to expanding and developing new programs that emerged from it. This has led us to propose a new Institute for Catholic Leadership in order to respond to the current crisis of leadership in the church and in civil society. This crisis strikes us as at once both grave and hopeful, grave in that it calls for a decisive response in the face of serious need, hopeful in that much can be accomplished as a new generation rises to the challenges before them. The institute will include a set of six programs that integrate intellectual and spiritual formation with residential living and career preparation. They include:

1. The Leadership Interns Program
2. Catholic Studies Community Living: Men's and Women's Houses and Residence Hall Floors
3. Professional Leadership Formation
4. The Latino Leadership Program
5. Catholic Studies Scholars Program
6. Post-doctoral Fellows Program

The institute will focus primarily on the formation of undergraduate students. To accomplish this work the institute will unite several existing Catholic Studies leadership initiatives with a number of new programs. In addition to assisting the formation of many young Catholic leaders, the institute also intends to become a place of thoughtful analysis concerning what it means to be a Catholic leader in the church and in civil society through publications, conferences, and scholar-in-residence programs so that its work can extend beyond our own campus.

Conclusion

Several years ago Tom Landy noted:

> While a Catholic Studies model is undoubtedly not the only way to develop an institution's Catholic identity, it can serve as an important means for developing Catholic identity within the academic program. . . . As David O'Brien has noted repeatedly, Catholic Studies programs increase the likelihood that Catholic colleges and universities can be places where the church can do its thinking and engage its own and other traditions. The next several years should prove a fruitful time for testing that possibility.[13]

---

13. Thomas M. Landy, "Catholic Studies at Catholic Colleges and Universities," in *Enhancing Religious Identity: Best Practices from Catholic Campuses*, ed. John Wilcox and Irene King (Washington, DC: Georgetown University Press, 2000) 225.

At St. Thomas, Catholic Studies has proven to be a remarkably vital academic project, one with wide and deep interest among students from varied intellectual backgrounds and career interests, with broad outreach to the local community in lectures, workshops, and symposia, with comprehensive faculty development programs and seminars providing forums for a sustained exploration of the implications of the Catholic intellectual tradition, with research projects and symposia, with a national quarterly journal exploring Catholic thought and culture, with international programs and study abroad opportunities, with student life, with residential and leadership formation programs, with collaborative programs with schools and colleges of the university, including joint degree programs, with partnership programs with the local church, with endowed lecture and visiting scholar programs, and with sustained engagement with professional and preprofessional programs both on and off campus.

In this work Catholic Studies at St. Thomas, as David O'Brien had predicted, has in significant ways served as a catalyst on campus for the renewal of the university's identity and mission. In doing so it has assisted the university in the task identified in the Land O'Lakes Statement of making Catholicism perceptibly present and effectively operative on our campus. The complexity and diversity of our institutions will increasingly require these kinds of interdisciplinary Catholic programs if we are to sustain a coherent vision of Catholic thought and culture for the wider university and for the broader culture.

_____ *Chapter 6* _____

A Pilgrimage to Rome

David Gentry-Akin

A s the student population of Catholic colleges and universities has changed over the years—increasingly being made up of fewer Catholics or at least of fewer Catholics with any real faith experience—I have been intrigued by the problem of how to teach theology, a discipline which always involves *fides quarens intellectum*, to young women and men who have the capacity for *intellectum* but who have no *fides*, or at least no *fides* experience. Because of ever-poorer backgrounds in the liberal arts, an increasingly heterogeneous student body made up of growing numbers of first-generation college students, and the pressure that rising costs place on young people to choose a field of study that will result in a good job or at least enable them to make the minimum monthly payment on their student loans, there is often great resistance to the study of theology. Many see no point in it. The theology requirement seems to be in place to meet the mission of the institution, but it does not, prima facie, respond to any "felt need" on the part of the student. Students seem to grasp the wisdom of the requirements of the core curriculum in Western civilization, composition, and the so-called breadth requirements in the humanities, math, the natural and social sciences, and so on, but as theology has increasingly been pushed to the margins of the curriculum, it seems less and less relevant to many students.

My readers are undoubtedly familiar with the problem and the challenges it poses for us as teachers of theology. I am as convinced as ever that the Catholic tradition and the Gospel it hands on have something of enormous value to offer our students. It is something our students desperately need and to which they will respond if it is presented in a way that captures their imaginations and inspires their intellects. But *how* to do that—amid all the challenges posed by the academy, the church, and the wider culture—is the question.

Mike Hayes, in *Googling God: The Religious Landscape of People in their 20s and 30s*, reminds us that "Millennial Young Adults," the "twenty-somethings" with whom we are now working, are often thought to be more "conservative," and, in terms of passing on a tradition concerned with conserving the wisdom of the past, that might be a good thing. However, he goes on to tell us that what looks like "conservatism" to older adults is, in fact, a longing for a contemplative experience and even for more demanding forms of faith.[1] Because they are living in a culture that bombards them with far more images than the psyche can process, they long for silence—for "spaces" without words or images—like eucharistic adoration. It is the lack of words and images that draws them to this form of prayer, more than some nostalgia for the devotions of the pre–Vatican II church. Their intense longing for certainty—something that adults working with them often find troubling—is both developmental and contextual. They inhabit a world in which the faith is no longer presented with the certainty that it once was, and a world that is at the same time far less stable geopolitically, and thus far less able to assure them of their own safety. Hayes points out that when Millennials talk about the history that has shaped their worldview, they talk about events like 9/11, the Columbine or Virginia Tech massacres, the Indian Tsunami, or Hurricane Katrina:

> As they construct the meaning of their stories, they recall the moments when terrorists flew planes into buildings, high school students shot their colleagues at random, and water took the lives and homes of entire cities. . . . In a world where life seems very fleeting, young adults search for things they can depend on, things that have stood the test of time, things they regard as true, and things that are greater than themselves."[2]

Hayes notes, "Faith for young adults is not a spectator sport. They long to integrate it into every fiber of their lives and live that faith unapologetically."[3]

For some time, the issue for me as a professor of theology has been how to structure learning experiences for young adults that will facilitate the process whereby they can "integrate [faith] into every fiber of their lives." My search led me to the conviction that the ancient wisdom about retreats—a wisdom that Jesus models with his disciples in the New Testament[4] and one

---

1. Mike Hayes, *Googling God: The Religious Landscape of People in their 20s and 30s* (New York: Paulist Press, 2007) 4.
2. Ibid., 4.
3. Ibid., 124.
4. See, for example, Mark 6:31: "He said to them, 'Come away by yourselves to a deserted place and rest a while.' People were coming and going in great numbers, and they had no opportunity even to eat. So they went off in the boat by themselves to a deserted place" (NAB).

that monastic communities and other spiritual movements in the Tradition have witnessed to throughout our history—could be a viable approach for young people. Days or weeks set apart, and in a milieu very different from the one of their everyday world, might facilitate experiences that allow students to transcend *kronos*, or mere time, and open themselves up to *kairos*, the appropriate moment. In other words, I came to the conviction that what many students need is a kind of immersion experience—something that will take them out of their typical environment, filled as it is with the distractions of other classes, part-time jobs, cell phones, e-mail—and place them in a rich milieu that might awaken or reawaken "faith experience" in them. Such an experience offers some of the elements of a retreat—a different environment, opportunities for prayer, for encounters with others who are on a similar journey—along with some of the classical components of a scholarly experience that would be both academically credible *and* creditable.

Walking in the Footsteps of the Early Christians

These reflections led me to develop a program, Walking in the Footsteps of the Early Christians: A Pilgrimage to Rome. The academic calendar at Saint Mary's College lends itself to these kinds of immersion experiences. We use what we call a 4–1–4 calendar that allows for a full January Term of four weeks during which students typically engage in travel courses and other immersion experiences. I also had a few years ago the good fortune of traveling to Rome to participate in the Rome Seminar: U.S. Catholic Higher Education in a Global Context, a weeklong experience sponsored by the Association of Catholic Colleges and Universities (ACCU) designed to give participants "a first-hand opportunity to explore the intellectual and spiritual legacy of the Catholic Church in order to strengthen and promote the mission of Catholic higher education in the United States."[5] During that rich experience, I was introduced to some wonderful people who live and work in Rome at the Lay Centre Foyer Unitas: Professor Donna Orsuto and her doctoral student Robert White, who would eventually become valued colleagues and whose collaboration on this course has been simply irreplaceable.[6] I was able to visit for the first time some of the sites that would eventually become integral to the course I envisioned. Finally, my idea was

5. To learn more about the Rome Seminar see: http://www.accunet.org/i4a/pages/index .cfm?pageid=3481.

6. The Lay Centre Foyer Unitas has a threefold mission that includes (1) offering programs for those living in Rome or coming from abroad for the purpose of exploring the theology, spirituality, history, and artistic treasures of Rome; (2) providing an international, residential community fostering the intellectual and spiritual growth of students enrolled in one of Rome's

able to move from vision to reality because of the presence in Rome of the motherhouse of the Brothers of the Christian Schools on Via Aurelia, just a couple of blocks from the Cornelia metro stop on the northwest end of the metro line, and just a few stops northwest of the Ottaviano stop, the stop just a short walk from Saint Peter's Square. The Brothers operate a hotel on the grounds of the motherhouse, "Casa La Salle", that offers clean, safe, monastic (read: no televisions!) accommodations to students and faculty, along with the ready availability of classrooms, a chapel, beautiful grounds, a museum dedicated to the life and works of the founder of the Christian Brothers, John Baptist de La Salle, and even the founder's relics.[7]

As presently structured, this course is a four-week experience. The first week takes place on the campus of Saint Mary's College, at the end of which the students and staff fly to Rome for a three-week residency. I recruit several others to serve as staff on the pilgrimage. This past year, they included a Dominican Sister of Mission San Jose, a Salvatorian priest, and a Christian Brother from my own institution. My goal is to surround the students with good mentors, all of whom are on a faith journey and yet have different stories and very different temperaments and lifestyles. I want the students to see a deeply held commitment to Catholic Christianity as a viable option for people of different backgrounds and lifestyles.

Students are recruited in September and begin preparations for the course with monthly meetings throughout the fall term. Early in the fall I assign the students three or four books consistent with the themes of the course.[8] Because of the Great Books seminar culture of Saint Mary's, students are accustomed to the expectation of substantial reading and seminar discussion. They choose roommates and sign up for the reading discussions they want to prepare to lead.

The first week after Christmas, back at Saint Mary's, consists of four 2.5-hour seminars during which we begin our text-based seminar discussions and make final preparations. Finally, on Sunday night, we gather to load the bus with our luggage for the trip to San Francisco International Airport, and then we all go to the Sunday night campus Eucharist to pray together and ask for God's blessing on our pilgrimage.

---

pontifical universities; (3) promoting Christian unity and interreligious dialogue. To learn more see: http://www.laycentre.org/.

7. To learn more about Casa La Salle see: http://www.casalasalle.com/.

8. For example, this past January students read and discussed J. J. Mueller et al, *Theological Foundations: Concepts and Methods for Understanding Christian Faith* (Winona, MN: Saint Mary's Press, 2007); Cyril C. Richardson, *Early Christian Fathers* (New York: Simon and Schuster, 1996); and Thomas E. Woods Jr., *How the Catholic Church Built Western Civilization* (Washington, DC: Regnery Publishing, 2005).

Once in Rome students settle into their rooms in the motherhouse, recover from jetlag, and get oriented to the motherhouse and to Rome: getting some sleep, changing currency, and so on. The following day our program begins in earnest. Each day has a theme and is shaped around four repeating elements: prayer (usually three times a day: an abbreviated form of Lauds and Vespers, the Morning and Evening Prayers of the church, and Mass), a lecture, a site visit, and seminar discussion. Add to this time for meals and free time and we have the ingredients for each day. The questions and themes with which the course deals are rich: the significance of Rome for early Christianity; the early Christian texts, beginning with Scripture and including the writings of the early Fathers and Mothers of the church, and the accounts of the martyrdom of significant figures like Polycarp and Perpetua; the contribution of the church to the building of Western culture; and the essential and yet rarely fully understood or appreciated Catholic approach to faith and reason. Other themes treated during our time in Rome include the theology of baptism, the role of women and house churches in early Christianity, the theology of martyrdom, the social justice tradition of the church, the role of art in Catholicism, and devotion to Mary, the Mother of God.

These rich themes are treated not merely through readings and lectures but through site visits that connect the ideas to concrete historical realities. In the early days of the course, we visit the magnificent Basilica of Saint Clement, a beautiful medieval structure built on the site of earlier Christian basilicas, which were themselves constructed over the site of a first-century Roman village thought to be the location of a house church led by Clement, the fourth bishop of Rome. The students gather for Lauds, or Morning Prayer, in this beautiful space and are treated to a thoughtful lecture on the astonishing apse mosaic. Including the crucifixion and other biblical scenes, the mosaic places biblical history into the context of the entire cosmos. The students are enthralled at the way in which the tree of death, the tree of the cross, has become the tree of life in the apse mosaic; at the way in which the blood coming from Jesus' side flows into a cup, which then flows into a fountain, which then becomes a river flowing out into the entire universe, nourishing the deer who drink from the fountain and nurturing the vine that becomes the source of life for all. In this virtually panentheistic vision of God's embrace of the whole universe, the students are reminded of the passage in the Gospel of John: "I am the vine, you are the branches. Whoever remains in me and I in him will bear much fruit, because without me you can do nothing"[9] They come to see that the Catholic vision of reality in-

---

9. See John 5:3b and ff. (NAB).

cludes suffering and death—because to omit the painful aspects of reality would be to construct a vision that is dishonest and can only be described as escapist. More importantly, however, they come to see that the shadow side of human experience, with all of its suffering and death, is brought into a much larger and all-encompassing vision that celebrates life, life in the here-and-now and life in eternity.

Another site that the students find deeply moving is that of the Catacombs of Saint Priscilla. As we wind our way down, down, down through the various levels of the catacomb and hear the stories of the early Christians who were buried there, the students come to realize in a palpable way that many, many generations of believers have walked the wisdom path of Catholic Christianity before them, that these believers were young and old, poor and rich, uneducated and educated, some remembered by name and others whose names are long forgotten. They gradually realize that these women and men have fascinating stories, that they lived lives of faith, commitment, and adventure that were far from boring. They come to appreciate more concretely that these men and women are the *saints*, that their lives and stories were real, that they were ordinary women and men drawn by a faith and a love so compelling that it gave them the psychological and spiritual strength to be able to pay the ultimate price—the sacrifice of their very lives—in witnessing to their faith. Finally, the students reach an open space with small rooms—possibly chapels where the Eucharist was celebrated in the early church—that are decorated with simple yet deeply beautiful images of the Good Shepherd, as well as depictions of the Three Young Men in the Fiery Furnace and of Jonah in the Belly of the Whale.

The students come to realize, day by day, that Catholic Christianity is much more than a set of abstract, intellectual propositions; instead it is an ongoing story, a drama into which they themselves are invited to step, and a living *traditio* that will survive if, and only if, it is lived, enfleshed, incarnated by each new generation and passed on to those who will come after us.

Toward the end of the course, we have the rare and intimate experience of visiting one of the Holy Father's private chapels within the Apostolic Palace: the exquisitely beautiful and highly contemporary Redemptoris Mater Chapel. It is only through the influence of Professor Orsuto that we are able to have the privilege of visiting this chapel, as it is one that only a few visitors to the Vatican ever have the opportunity to experience. Commissioned with a gift that John Paul II received from the College of Cardinals on the occasion of his fiftieth anniversary of ordination, this chapel is in the shape of a cube and has a rounded ceiling that creates the feeling for the visitor of being in a womb-like space. The walls—front, back, sides, and ceiling—are decorated with incredible mosaics that tell the story of salvation and give the viewer a sense of God in Christ "coming down" to earth, embracing humanity, and "rising up" again to heaven, which results in a feeling of the viewers themselves being caught up in the drama.

The official description of the chapel verifies that this feeling was, in fact, intended by the artists and is, indeed, good theology: "God made human, [as one who has fully] entered into our human and cosmic reality. Because of this, our hope is not in heaven, but in a heaven on earth, the reign of God among us."[10] A magnificent image of Christ, the Pantokrator, the universal king of the cosmos and of all time—dressed in vivid red (for divinity) and blue (for humanity)—adorns the ceiling. Images of the heavenly Jerusalem, the incarnation of the Word, and Christ the Salvation of Humankind fill the space. Salvation is, in fact, depicted as having been achieved by Christ's presence in the "womb" of Mary at his human birth, the "womb" of the Jordan at his baptism, and the "womb" of the tomb at his death. The ascension of the Lord and the coming of the Holy Spirit are depicted in such a way as to represent the mystery of the divinization of humanity and of its eventual reunion with the Father. The sense of a dynamic unfolding of salvation history continuing into our own day is reinforced with images of contemporary martyrs like Edith Stein, a Jewish woman who converted to Catholicism, became a Carmelite nun, and later died in the gas chamber at Auschwitz; as well as Marija Shveda, a Greco-Catholic Ukrainian who was a victim of the Russian persecution; and Elisabeth von Thadden, a German Lutheran who was also a victim of the Nazi persecution.

Other elements of our pilgrimage include a papal audience with the Holy Father in the Paul VI Audience Hall at the Vatican; an opportunity to pray with the pope and leaders of other Christian traditions at the conclusion of the Week of Prayer for Christian Unity—the Feast of the Conversion of Saint Paul—at the beautiful basilica of Saint Paul Outside the Walls, in the crypt where the apostle Paul is believed to have been buried; an encounter with the post–Vatican II lay community of Sant'Egidio, including participation in the beautiful, Taizé-like Vespers they pray each night in the Church of Santa Maria in Trastevere;[11] and guided tours of the Basilica of San Pietro, the Cathedral of San Giovanni Laterano, and the Basilica of Santa Maria Maggiore. We stay in Rome for the entire three weeks with the exception

10. See "Salvation History" under the Theological Tour on the chapel's web site: http://www.vatican.va/redemptoris_mater/index_en.htm.

11. This church is the oldest church dedicated to Mary in the entire world. It is packed with people—young and old, from near and far—for the Sant'Egidio Vespers service every night, which is available in numerous languages via simultaneous translation.

of one or two day trips: one to Assisi, the land of Clare and Francis, and the other to Subiaco, where Benedict first embraced monastic life as a hermit.

This experience, and others like it, leave the students "immersed" and "swimming" in an ocean of stories and images, of people living and dead, of art and music—a multisensory experience of sight, sound, smell, taste, and touch—that inspires them deeply, that brings the Catholic Christian vision of reality to life, that awakens a great many more questions and, hopefully, arouses yearnings within the students that will motivate them to continue their exploration of the Christian mystery when they return home. The students love the experience of living in the same location in Rome for three weeks, and of really getting to know the city. They come to have a dramatically different take on Catholic Christianity, beginning to grasp that it is not simply a religion with lots of sanctions about sex and other fun activities, but rather a compelling vision of reality, probably the most compelling vision to which they have ever been exposed. They love the experience of unity that transcends so many cultures, languages, races, and geographic regions when the Holy Father comes into the Paul VI Audience Hall and people are chanting *Viva il Papa*, when groups of school children or elderly pilgrims are acknowledged and they rise to sing a simple melody for the pope, and they witness his complete attention on them and his gratitude for their gesture. On our last visit, the students were acknowledged as a group by the master of ceremonies, and they were able to rise and sing the simple Taizé melody *Magnificat* for the pope. Honestly, it was as if they were completely intoxicated by the experience for the next twenty-four hours.

Processing the Experience

While the rationalists among us might dismiss the whole experience as a mere emotional indulgence, I would argue that the students did indeed have a deeply emotional experience, one that conveyed some profound learning that will take them years to fully unpack and process. For example, on the metro going to Saint Paul's for Vespers with the Holy Father on the Feast of the Conversion of Saint Paul, they were amazed at the extraordinary popularity of the event, the excitement it generated, the packed trains, the eagerness and fervor of the people queued up for hours in order to get tickets, much like their friends would do before a Bruce Springsteen concert.

They were amazed at the sheer diversity of the Catholic Church: the presence of so many priests, brothers, and sisters from all over the world, many of them quite young, many of them in diverse, colorful, and curious religious habits—from the simple and almost universally recognized saris of Mother Teresa's Missionaries of Charity to the Polish nun, complete with the traditional habit and whimple that made her look exactly like the kind of nun that one might have encountered in a Catholic School of the 1950s, something most of the students had never witnessed before.

The students were continuously amazed at the way that life and religion bled into one another in Rome: the way they could go into a bar to order a beer and find pictures of the Sacred Heart, the Blessed Mother, and the Pope on the wall behind the bar, adjacent to the bottles of beer, wine, or whiskey. Or the way they could go—when in a completely different frame of mind— into a religious goods store to purchase a rosary for their moms back home and find the music of "Madonna" (and here we are most emphatically not talking about the Mother of our Lord!) playing in the background. They were so used to compartmentalizing religion that the permeable boundary they found between religious experience and the rest of life in Rome became quite disarming, puzzling, even a little troubling. They came to recognize that religion and faith function quite differently in Italian/Roman culture and it took them a while to assimilate that.

Again, my goal is to help students move from American secular culture's portrayal of religion as something for the weak, something for those who need excessive structure and rules, to a deeper grasp of the richly compelling culture and life vision of Catholic Christianity.

Thomas Rausch notes how crucial it is to help young adults grasp that Catholicism is not merely a religion experienced by "going to church" but a deeply layered, complex, and compelling vision of reality:

> Catholicism is not just a particular church or Christian tradition; it is a way of life, a way of seeing the world, rooted in . . . the Catholic sacramental imagination. A Catholic imagination does not restrict God's grace to the sacramental symbols and ritual moments. It includes more than the explicitly religious. Because it takes its fundamental inspiration from the doctrine of the incarnation, it recognizes that God's grace is abundantly present in creation and the genuinely human.[12]

Upon their return home, students wrote an integration paper about their experience, combining insights from the assigned texts with reflections on their experience. Their comments made it clear that they had a rich experience of Catholic Christianity, one that enabled them to grasp that "[b]eing Catholic means being a part of God's people, a disciple of Jesus, a member of his body, the Church. If the Catholic Church is not the whole of the

---

12. Thomas P. Rausch, *Being Catholic in a Culture of Choice* (Collegeville, MN: Liturgical Press, 2006) 117.

Church, it has a unique claim to antiquity, catholicity, and apostolicity."[13] One of the recent participants in this pilgrimage described his experience in this way:

> What the [pilgrimage to Rome] has meant to me is this amazing and surprising sense of pure, almost transcendent unity that affected us all when we saw the Holy Father. When we went to the Papal Audience Hall, we encountered all of these people from all over the world acknowledging the pope and the unity that he represents, but doing that in their own unique way, according to their own diverse cultures. I was moved by the way that the Holy Father—obviously quite an intelligent and sophisticated man— acknowledged each of the groups of pilgrims with a simplicity and a joy that seemed to border on the childlike. That all of these people—in spite of the strife and conflict that humans continually experience with one another—could converge on this holy place and feel totally at peace with each other, even for a few moments, is utterly astonishing to me. All of us in our group experienced this incredibly hopeful feeling from this event. As a result, all of us began to develop a very strong bond with one other; eventually everyone knew everyone, no one wanted to leave anyone behind, and we began to really care about each other. That is really what the trip to Rome has meant to me: an amazing unity existing in the midst of all of our differences and distinctions. I think that perhaps what I experienced is a pure gift of grace.[14]

Conclusion

Reading these comments and those of the other students led me back to a very profound text that has nevertheless not received much attention in American Catholic higher education. I am speaking of Pope Benedict XVI's beautiful and moving remarks to Catholic educators on the occasion of his apostolic visit to the United States in April 2008. In those remarks, the Holy Father writes:

> Truth means more than knowledge: knowing the truth leads us to discover the good. Truth speaks to the individual in his or her entirety, inviting us to respond with our whole being. This optimistic vision is found in our Christian faith because such faith has been granted the vision of the *Logos*, God's creative Reason, which in the Incarnation, is revealed as Goodness itself. Far from being just a communication of factual data—"informative"— the loving truth of the Gospel is creative and life-changing—"performative" (cf. *Spe Salvi*, 2). With confidence, Christian educators can liberate the

---

13. Ibid.
14. In an e-mail dated February 2, 2009, and quoted with permission.

young from the limits of positivism and awaken receptivity to the truth, to God and his goodness. In this way you will also help to form their conscience which, enriched by faith, opens a sure path to inner peace and to respect for others. . . . Once their passion for the fullness and unity of truth has been awakened, young people will surely relish the discovery that the question of what they can know opens up the vast adventure of what they ought to do. Here they will experience "in what" and "in whom" it is possible to hope, and be inspired to contribute to society in a way that engenders hope in others.[15]

Hopefully, this course is making a small contribution toward inspiring faith and hope for the future in the Catholic young adults with whom I work at Saint Mary's College of California.

15. For the full text of this splendid address see: http://www.vatican.va/holy_father/
benedict_xvi/speeches/2008/april/documents/hf_ben-xvi_spe_20080417_cath
-univ-washington_en.html.

Chapter 7

Community-Based Learning

Kristin E. Heyer

Community-based learning (CBL) combines organized service activities with guided reflection and critical analysis to enhance both the academic objectives of the curriculum and the social needs of the larger community. Ultimately, CBL courses strive to cultivate solidarity between the university and the wider social context in which it is located, whereby community members, students, faculty, and institutions are mutually transformed by this collaborative pedagogy. In terms of transformative education in the Jesuit tradition, CBL presents one particularly promising method for letting "the gritty reality of this world into students' lives" such that they can critically respond to and engage suffering in a globalized context.[1] Hence CBL well serves an Ignatian pedagogy that puts academic rigor at the service of meeting the world's needs and promoting human flourishing.

As a theologian who teaches in the area of Catholic social ethics, I have come to highly value CBL pedagogy for the role it plays in educating students for solidarity with the marginalized. At a basic level, incorporation of CBL has brought my course texts and concepts to life by engaging students in their social contexts beyond the ivory tower (or in the case of our university, beyond the bluffs overlooking the Pacific Ocean), thereby expanding and breaking open students' experience of learning about immigration or environmental racism. Such experiences drive home the urgency of theological and ethical

---

1. Peter-Hans Kolvenbach, "The Service of Faith and the Promotion of Justice in American Jesuit Higher Education," Santa Clara University, October 6, 2000, available at http://74.125.95.132/search?q=cache:lJ7F7cb8ICwJ:www.scu.edu/ignatiancenter/events/conferences/archives/justice/upload/f07_kolvenbach_keynote.pdf+Peter-Hans+Kolvenbach,+S.J.,+%E2%80%9CThe+Service+of +Faith+and+the+Promotion+of+Justice+in+American+Jesuit+Higher+Education,%E2%80%9D&hl=en&ct=clnk&cd=1&gl=us&client=firefox-a.

reflection and action on contemporary social issues: cycles of domestic abuse and chronic homelessness become more pressing in the concrete, for example. In general I have also found the experiential dimension of these courses helps counter student apathy, a tendency to privatize ethical issues typical of the millennial generation, and an entrenched resistance to structural analyses. The documents of the Thirty-Fifth General Congregation of the Jesuits discuss the growing paradoxes and tensions of globalization in ways that CBL is particularly suited to help students, community partners, and faculty address: "We live in a culture that shows partiality to autonomy and the present, and yet we have a world so much in need of building a future in solidarity; we have better ways of communication but often experience isolation and exclusion; some have greatly benefited while others have been marginalized and excluded."[2] Human encounters in students' service placement experiences often serve to embody these trends in ways that course texts illuminating contemporary patterns or urging globalization without marginalization cannot.

Transformative Pedagogy in Christian Ethics

I have taught three different CBL courses in my Jesuit and Marymount University[3] setting: an upper level core course entitled "Catholic Social Teaching and Action," which also serves the Catholic Studies minor, and two undergraduate seminars for theological studies majors and minors: "Christian Ethics and Social Responsibility" and "Christian Ethics and HIV/AIDS." Since each course in part considers particular social implications of Christian theology and ethics and takes as its starting point the conciliar charge to dialogically engage these contemporary realities,[4] it makes sense that students directly engage relevant signs of the times. CBL components not only highlight the significance of the tradition of Christian social ethics as a living one and reality as a significant source and conversation partner, but also help introduce students to "signs of hope." During my

2. General Congregation 35, Decree 3, paragraph 11 (2008), available at http://www.sjweb .info/35/documents/Decrees.pdf.

3. The courses discussed herein were taught at Loyola Marymount University from 2003–09.

4. "This Council can provide no more eloquent proof of its solidarity with the entire human family with which it is bound up, as well as its respect and love for that family, than by engaging with it in conversation about these various problems" (*Gaudium et spes* [Pastoral Constitution on the Church in the Modern World], no. 3, in *The Documents of Vatican II*, ed. Walter M. Abbott (New York: America Press, 1966).

initial years teaching Christian ethics I have become aware of undergraduates' tendencies to become overwhelmed by the enormity of the world's injustices or paralyzed by their complicity in structural sins. It has become important for my courses to move beyond conscientization of students toward their empowerment for working for positive change by highlighting cases of thriving community organizing groups or fair trade cooperatives and having students work alongside volunteers and mentors who may serve as signs of hope.

I typically require students to complete twenty hours of service throughout the semester in carefully selected placements where they can develop relationships over time with socially oppressed and marginalized persons. In my experience CBL courses rise or fall on the ability of professors to effectively facilitate meaningful integration of students' classroom-based and community-based experiences. I attempt to accomplish this by means of integration papers or journal assignments, guided in-class discussions, and monitoring students' placement experiences via periodic evaluations and ongoing dialogue with students and community partners. Integration paper prompts require students to synthesize their textual and classroom learning with their community experiences: they might ask students to identify which human rights are being violated for the clients at their placement and then articulate how a classically liberal paradigm would assess and address those violations compared to a personalist communitarian model. A subsequent assignment might ask students to identify which social sins are operative in the situations that have given rise to these human rights violations or the needs they are helping meet at their placement. The final evaluation of one of my core students illustrates the value of these encounters:

> While we discussed the intersections of modern injustices with Jesus's gospel of love for the poor and marginalized in my Catholic Social Teaching class, the most significant experience I had through this class was volunteering weekly at Guadalupe Homeless Project, a homeless shelter primarily for immigrant men from Latin America, where I witnessed some of these injustices first-hand. At Dolores Mission, the "service" work we did included checking the men in, setting the tables for dinner, and even teaching English at times, yet the most important thing that we did there, in fact, was to simply talk with the men and listen to their stories. Through my interactions with the men, I heard about the challenges they faced as strangers living in a foreign country, and in them I saw the face of homelessness; I saw the face of immigration. These experiences forced me to become aware of the human rights violations and social injustices that we talked about in class but that these men faced in their daily lives.

Guided seminar discussions also help facilitate students' integration of these distinct loci of learning. In one of my AIDS class discussions I had students engage such questions as:

> How might sensitivity to the suffering persons you encounter in your placement impact your image of God?

> What light does your experience shed on the anthropological question of what human life means or the humanum?

> How might your own concrete AIDS-related experiences bring new questions to current principles of Catholic moral theology? How would such responses remain faithful to the prophetic/Jesus tradition as Musa Dube articulates it? To Raphael Gallagher's understanding of how and why a tradition develops? To Enda McDonagh's understanding of the Reign of God marked by kenosis, compassion, justice, inclusion and Jesus' "risk-laden" example?

Finally, the incorporation of a final integration project in my core course provides students with an opportunity to integrate their CBL experiences with the whole of the course as a culminating project. This offers students a chance to directly draw upon their skills and in many cases their major disciplines and to complete the hermeneutical circle around which the course is designed with some sort of integrative praxis. I have been rather impressed by the substance and creativity marking the final integration projects each semester, ranging from well-researched letters to members of Congress; to engineering students' bilingual energy conservation brochures showing how St. Margaret's Center clients could save money on utility bills based on detailed water, gas, and lighting analyses; to professional-quality multimedia presentations bringing course themes to life. Many of the students most skeptical about the service component entering the course ultimately rise to the challenge of bringing their own skills to meet needs identified through the course's experiential learning dimension. Students who opt to write a social analysis paper instead of completing a praxis project must also engage the community in an in-depth manner in the course of their investigation.

Reflecting upon my experiences with this pedagogy, I discovered that CBL has deepened and sharpened my teaching as well as moved students beyond my own courses in some significant ways. To begin with, service among the most marginalized often challenges students' very paradigms for understanding social problems and their solutions. Throughout the various CBL courses I have taught, my students' experiences with former gang members in East Los Angeles or grade-school children in Watts have prompted them to challenge unexamined assumptions about the causes of poverty, migration, or even "criminal activity." Dean Brackley aptly terms these opportunities to "act ourselves into new ways of thinking" *cognitive hygiene*, emphasizing that "we must be engaged at the level of experience and practice in a way that challenges our intellectual and moral commitments."[5] CBL drives home the urgency of reflection and action on contemporary social issues, for building relationships makes it harder to generalize about groups of people. Accompanying undocumented immigrants facing daunting language barriers or recognizing the same families week after week at a food bank impacts students' thinking on structural dimensions of justice. This is an essential step in negotiating the tensions that often persist between students' inherited assumptions and perspectives informed by Christian commitments. For, according to Brackley, "we are naïve if we suppose that reason alone can take us to [personal transformation]. Affectivity and commitment, which are central to the problem of distortion, are, logically enough, crucial to [cognitive liberation] also."[6] My teaching experiences repeatedly bear out Brackley's claims.

Hence community-based learning can confound students' expectations and loyalties in fruitful ways. As the founder of the PULSE Program for Service Learning at Boston College has reflected, as a result of students' placements, "[t]hey encounter intransigence where their paradigms expect success; they find happiness, freedom, creativity and love where their paradigms predict none. These field encounters provide irreplaceable stimuli for paradigm change."[7] When I taught in BC's PULSE program as a graduate student, one undergraduate admitted in a journal entry that even if the promising kids she tutored at a downtown shelter worked hard and played by the rules, they would always have significantly fewer opportunities through no fault of their own. This realization challenged her insistence on an "even playing field" at a very concrete and affective level, in a way that up to that point our theology and philosophy texts had not. In this sense CBL frequently decenters the professor in ways that can challenge the comfort level of faculty, just as the location and clientele of placements may initially disrupt the comfort level of their students.

Moving Beyond the Confines of Coursework

Beyond the "paradigm subverting" purposes they may accomplish, CBL can help lead students to new perspectives on other disciplines and links

---

5. Dean Brackley, "Higher Standards for Higher Education: The Christian University and Solidarity," available at http://www.marquette.edu/library/subjects/mission.html.

6. Ibid.

7. Patrick H. Byrne, "Paradigms of Justice and Love," *Conversations in Jesuit Higher Education*, 7 (Spring 1995), available at http://www.marquette.edu/library/collections/archives/Conversations/No7_1995/No7_byrne.PDF.

between disciplines, a fruitful end given the fragmentation and disintegration that characterizes most undergraduate curricula. My students' placement experiences raise questions that draw upon their coursework in economics, psychology, political science, urban planning, and communications—crucial to a comprehensive approach to issues of injustice and to holistic education. CBL also helps bridge the gap between student life and academic life, spheres typically compartmentalized. The integration of CBL in my theological ethics courses has also helped students to understand the interconnections between faith and justice and between academic reflection and social action more generally.

In addition to such interdisciplinary and cocurricular integration, I find praxis opportunities often prompt students to probe their self-understanding, vocation, and enduring questions of meaning. The reflections of a student in my core course on Catholic social thought offer one illustration:

> My placement at Guadalupe Homeless Project fundamentally transformed my idea of service. Not only were abstract concepts from class such as social sin, human dignity, and solidarity made real through personal interactions, but I was also deeply filled by the humanity of the men who shared their stories with me. Through weekly visits, service became a simple meeting of people and building of community. Physically and materially we can only do so much, I realized, but when we attend to the humanity of a person, we are able to care for one another in a deeper way. Every time I went to GHP, I found in the stranger a brother, a father, a friend, and I saw God working profoundly in us all through the relationships built there. Over time, I discovered that accompanying people through their struggles is the first step to working toward greater change, that growing in relationship with those who suffer—the homeless, the poor, the migrants—draws me closer to social issues of homelessness, poverty, immigration. Even now, these social ills have become personal to me and pull at my heart because the problem is no longer an abstract idea in the distance but profoundly affects individuals who are close to me. By being with people through their struggles, I find that I am bound up in this struggle with them, and their suffering pulls me into their fight for a better life.

In terms of ways in which CBL components can ignite vocational questions for students, one recent graduate from my core course was hired at her service placement, Good Shepherd Battered Women's Shelter, after graduation; another student stayed on as a caseworker at St. Joseph's homeless service center; yet another began offering weekly ESL classes at Guadalupe Homeless Project after the course requirement concluded. Two students who took my AIDS seminar were inspired to build upon their interests in dimensions of the pandemic that the CBL component highlighted, in particular:

[In Christian Ethics and HIV/AIDS] I learned that those who suffer from HIV undergo immense physical pain, but they also suffer from social stigmatization, gender inequality, and economic marginalization. These less acknowledged truths were illustrated in the course readings, but they received a human face through the service component of the course. Each week I sat in a support group for Latinas infected or affected by HIV/AIDS through an organization called Bienestar. As a participant, I heard and witnessed the reality of AIDS in my own community. I learned to question my own uninformed perspectives while gaining compassion for transgender individuals. This experience allowed my understanding of AIDS to develop from a medical dilemma haunting the third world into an injustice affecting my friends which called for my personal response. I came to realize that AIDS and the suffering it fosters are fueled by countless social sins—misconstrued gender roles, uncontested religious norms, and political apathy.

Learning about this in the classroom and acknowledging it in the community, I developed a passion to use my new knowledge to create change. My fellow classmate and I lived in Mexico City the following summer as interns for an NGO which provides outreach to HIV+ women throughout Mexico. We helped develop a program at the International AIDS Conference to create dialogue on the intersection between gender inequality and vulnerability to HIV. We are currently leading female empowerment outreach to youth in East Los Angeles to counter the societal norms which encourage HIV infections. The challenging experience we had listening to the stories of HIV+ individuals while studying the issue in books yielded our desire to prevent similar stories in the future.

Conclusion

Accompanying students along these cocurricular paths can be both humbling and daunting, particularly where CBL placement experiences trigger students to question career paths they (and their parents) had taken for granted or challenge students' received religious worldview. In my AIDS seminar, another student's service placement in the aforementioned Latino outreach program prompted sincere faith exploration outside of the classroom. As she put it in her CBL presentation to the seminar,

> I feel almost like I don't know what to believe anymore. When I was growing up, the decision was always already made for me—what did my parents say—which was whatever the Church said. But now I feel like I don't know what to think. Because things aren't as cut and dry anymore. Not when I read about the millions who are innocently given a death sentence because a condom wasn't used. Or when I go to Bienestar and meet with the people and see their loneliness, frustrations, disordered self-image . . . what does love say? What does compassion say? Jesus ate with the outcasts

of society. He said the healthy do not need a doctor but the sick do. What if these people are just spiritually, humanly hungry, lonely? Can the Church, the Body of Christ, the people, fix this? Is this not what the Church is called to do? Are these marginalized persons not our *anawim*?

This student engaged in sustained conversations with her companions in prayer, other peers, and with me regarding the implications of what she was experiencing in the course for her faith life.

This final example of a student whose placement initially caused personal discomfort yet who persevered and genuinely wrestled with intersecting layers of the issues the experiences surfaced well illustrates the impact CBL can have on students' intellectual and spiritual development. Beyond enabling students to concretely confront the realities facing suffering or marginalized persons and the values that facilitate theological reflection, the interdisciplinary integration and vocational or personal discernment occasioned by CBL experiences indicate the pedagogy's contribution to enduring goals of transformative education.

Chapter 8

Praxis-Based Education

Mark Ravizza, S.J.

In a talk at Santa Clara University in 2000, the superior general of the Society of Jesus, Father Peter-Hans Kolvenbach set forth a new standard for higher education. Without wanting to dismiss the importance of academic excellence and moral formation, he insisted that these alone were not enough in a world characterized by great injustice and profound human pain. "We must therefore raise our Jesuit educational standard to 'educate the whole person of solidarity for the real world,'" [1] Father Kolvenbach announced. He went on to explain that forming such solidarity required a personal immersion into the lived reality of those who suffer most:

> Solidarity is learned through "contact" rather than through "concepts."
> . . . Personal involvement with innocent suffering, with the injustice others suffer, is the catalyst for solidarity, which then gives rise to intellectual inquiry and moral reflection.
>
> Students, in the course of their formation, must let the gritty reality of this world into their lives, so they can learn to feel it, think about it critically, respond to its suffering, and engage it constructively. They should learn to perceive, think, judge, choose, and act for the rights of others, especially the disadvantaged and the oppressed. [2]

Father Kolvenbach's remarks made "praxis-based learning" [3] a central and indispensable component of Jesuit higher education. Yet in setting this

---

1. Peter-Hans Kolvenbach, "The Service of Faith and the Promotion of Justice in Jesuit Higher Education," in *A Jesuit Education Reader*, ed. George W. Traub (Chicago: Loyola Press, 2008) 155.

2. Ibid.

3. Although this term admits of a variety of interpretations, in the context of this essay I would like to use it to refer specifically to the type of learning championed in Father Kolvenbach's address—i.e., "intellectual inquiry and moral reflection" rooted in direct contact with

new standard he did not intend to break with tradition but rather to adapt long-held goals of Jesuit humanistic education to the realities of the twenty-first century. The first Jesuit universities were founded, in part, to promote the common good and produce graduates who were *maxime humanissimi* (most fully human).[4] The hope was that students benefiting from a humanistic education would "spread the good accomplished to many others who are under their influence" and "become laborers for the help of others."[5] Father Kolvenbach's stress on praxis-based learning can be seen as a new extension of this old tradition. It is the natural result of asking how today's students can learn to work for the common good and become "most fully human" in an increasingly globalized world marked by injustice and a growing disparity between rich and poor. As the Jesuit scholar Michael Buckley has argued, humanistic education today demands more than "the education of the mind, affectivity, and sensibility in the great achievements of the human being. . . . It must also denote the humane development into a deeper sensitivity and understanding of the lot of the wretched within our world and an affective longing and commitment to enter into the healing of human pain."[6]

In this chapter, I would like to explore some of the strategies, benefits, and challenges of praxis-based learning. The immediate context for my reflection is the experience of teaching and accompanying students for the past several years at the *Casa de la Solidaridad* in El Salvador. The *Casa* is a study-abroad program sponsored by Santa Clara University that integrates direct immersion among the poor with rigorous academic study.[7] Students spend two days a week volunteering in marginal Salvadoran communities (called "praxis sites"); their course work, in turn, revolves around reflecting on their experience accompanying the poor and studying the factors that give rise to this reality. In addition, the students participate in an integrated program of formation and community life that includes weekly spirituality

---

"innocent suffering" and "injustice," with the aim of fostering a well-educated solidarity, especially with "the disadvantaged and oppressed."

4. For an excellent discussion of Christian humanism and Jesuit education, see Michael J. Buckley, "Christian Humanism and Human Misery: A Challenge to the Jesuit University," in *Faith, Discovery, Service: Perspectives on Jesuit Education*, ed. Francis M. Lazarus (Milwaukee: Marquette University Press, 1992) 77–105.

5. *The Constitutions of the Society of Jesus and Their Complementary Norms* (St. Louis: Institute of Jesuit Sources, 1996), no. 622.

6. Buckley, "Christian Humanism and Human Misery," 98.

7. Educating students from North America is only one aspect of the *Casa* program. In addition, it provides housing and formation for Salvadoran scholarship students and works with the community partners in the local praxis sites. Unfortunately, a full description of the *Casa* program is beyond the scope of this essay.

nights and community nights, weekend retreats, and opportunities for individual accompaniment and spiritual direction.

At the *Casa*, I teach a course entitled "The Philosophy of Suffering and Solidarity." A central aim of the course is to help students develop an intellectual framework to interpret their experiences in El Salvador and to articulate how these experiences are changing them. Using a variety of sources, including philosophical and theological essays, film, and literature, the course examines how one critically engages experiences of interconnection, solidarity, and suffering, and uses such experiences to discern one's vocation and calling. In what follows, I would like to discuss four dimensions that facilitate praxis-based learning in the class: (1) Academic Reflection Rooted in Reality, (2) Integrated Community Learning, (3) Recollection and Pedagogical Accompaniment, and (4) Formation of a Christic Imagination.

Academic Reflection Rooted in Reality

The most important aspect of the *Casa* program is the connection the students form with the Salvadoran people. Being welcomed into their homes and lives, being invited into their joys and sufferings, being moved by their faith and generosity, these experiences prompt questions and transform students in ways that few academic texts can. As Father Kolvenbach has said, "when the heart is touched by direct experience, the mind may be challenged to change."[8] To illustrate this point, consider the following story that a student, Susan, shared after visiting the house of a poor family in her praxis site:

> The mother of the family, Oti, and I were cooking lunch. The night before,
> I had been bitten all over by bugs, and as the kitchen grew hotter, my legs
> started to itch like crazy. The more I scratched, the worse they got. When
> Oti looked down and saw my legs covered with swollen, red bug bites, she
> told me that she had a little medicine, a "special ointment," that she had
> been saving since some visitors had given it to her a few years ago. She
> went into her bedroom and returned with a small tube of cream half full.
> I put out my hand expecting that she would give me a bit of the lotion to
> put on my legs. But instead, Oti squeezed the entire tube into her own two
> hands, and then got down on her knees and began to massage the cream
> gently into my burning skin.[9]

8. Kolvenbach, "The Service of Faith and the Promotion of Justice," 155.

9. I am grateful to my students for allowing me to share their stories. Some are adapted from conversations in class, others from their journals and papers. In all cases, I have changed names and details to respect the privacy of those involved.

As Susan told this story in class, she shared that she could not get this moment out of her mind. In particular she kept asking herself:

> Why did I assume that Oti would just put a drop of lotion in my hand? And why, instead, did she put everything she had into her own hands, and then lavish it so generously on me? The cream was a gift she had been saving for months. She doesn't have the money to buy more. I didn't deserve it or have any right to it, and yet for Oti this was the only natural thing to do. Why do I see the world so differently than she does?

Susan's question became an opportunity to deepen a conversation that we had been having earlier in class comparing an "ethics of justice" with an "ethics of care."[10] Discussing her example, our theoretical analysis took on new meaning as the students reflected on how they tended to see the world though the lens of individual rights and duties, and how their imaginations were shaped by the individualism that flows from certain social contract models. As they contrasted this perspective with the communitarian sense of care they found in their praxis sites, they began to debate different conceptions of social justice. This in turn led to a rich discussion about the difference between "fairness" and "solidarity" in the parable of the Laborers in the Vineyard (Matt 20:1-16). I had taught this material many times before, but it came to life in a new way when it was energized by real questions flowing from the students' genuine need to make sense of their own experience.

Susan's story gives just one example of how praxis experience can enhance theoretical reflection. There are hundreds more, and yet this very richness points not only to the benefits of experiential education but also to one of its challenges. One never knows how a student will be touched by reality. This makes incorporating praxis experience particularly challenging. Unlike a traditional course where one can choose the texts, know their content, and introduce them at the proper moment in the semester, one cannot predict what will arise at a praxis site or how it might transform a student. In some cases, as in the example of Susan, praxis experience integrates nicely with the course material under discussion, but just as often, a student's experience will require the instructor to let go of a carefully crafted lesson plan. At other times, students may have significant moments at their praxis site but not recognize how these connect with class material. For this reason, I have found it useful to give students weekly journal assignments, asking them to reflect on their praxis experiences in the light of specific questions

---

10. See Annette Baier, "The Need for More than Justice," *Canadian Journal of Philosophy*, supplementary vol. 13, ed. Marshal Hanen and Kai Nielsen (Calgary: University of Calgary Press, 1986) 41–56.

that are framed in terms of the theological and philosophical concepts being discussed that week. An added advantage of this approach is that over time it has enabled me to assemble a collection of "praxis stories" that I have correlated with each topic in the class. Just as Susan's story of Oti elicited a host of examples from other students, so I use the praxis stories from previous years to stimulate students to see their own experiences in a new light. This regular practice of storytelling frequently becomes the part of class where students make the most profound, and personal, connections between theory and praxis.

A further challenge of praxis-based learning stems from the way it engages personal issues from the students' own history. When I first heard Father Kolvenbach's address, I had a simpler, more linear picture, of how praxis experiences would lead students to form a well-educated solidarity. I imagined that direct "contact" with those most in need would open their eyes to "innocent suffering." This, in turn, would raise questions about "injustice" and prompt students to engage in the "intellectual inquiry and moral reflection" needed to analyze the structural problems, and respond in ways that made the world a better place. While I still believe that at times this does happen, the more I use praxis experiences in my courses, the more I have come to see that educating students to be in solidarity is a far more complex process than I once imagined. In particular, when the students have direct contact with "gritty reality," it is never just about the reality of the poor. Engagement with their lives elicits profound questions about the students' own lives. Contact with innocent suffering surfaces their own pain. For example, consider this account from Julie, who was drawn to a "sad, lonely, and scared" teenager as they talked by the river at her praxis site:

> In that moment, Maria reminded me of myself. Though Maria and I lead completely different lives, I saw in her the inability to communicate that had held me back from happiness my entire life. . . . I looked at her and told her that I could see the sadness in her eyes, even if she thought she was fooling everyone else. In that moment, tears began to well up in her eyes, though she was quick to wipe them dry. Little by little, she began to speak—never revealing too much, and always making sure to hide her tears in fear that her family would see. Watching Maria's silent struggle it was as if I was seeing myself for the first time. Little by little, she began to tell me that she had no one she could talk to—or rather, she did not feel she could talk to anyone even if she tried . . . but she risked talking to me. . . .
>
> After hearing Maria's struggle with her family, I began to share with her parts of my own story. As we walked back from the river, I found myself telling her details of my life that I had yet to share with anyone else.

Julie's story is not unique. Indeed, I have come to believe that many students are attracted to programs like the *Casa* that explicitly engage suffering because they themselves are suffering, and they are seeking (perhaps unconsciously) venues where such pain and heartbreak can be addressed. These students are especially able to reach out to Salvadorans who are struggling through problems analogous to their own. In this way, their own history of suffering gives them a privileged way to connect, often despite great language barriers. Because these connections not only underscore the injustice the students observe around them but also surface their own brokenness, they tend to play a significant role in the students' growth and transformation. Course work has an important part to play in this process, especially insofar as it addresses questions of suffering, theodicy, and discernment. Yet, course work needs to be supplemented by a spectrum of other programmatic features, and this makes integration vitally important at the *Casa*.

Integrated Community Learning

One of the great strengths of the *Casa* program is that it approaches education not on a course-by-course basis but rather by conceptualizing the students' learning in terms of an integrated web of shared experiences, ranging from praxis sites and classroom discussions to community life and weekend outings. Sharing this common structure encourages students to reflect on course material throughout the day. For example, theological ideas from class frequently take on deeper meaning in individual spiritual direction, retreats, and spirituality nights; concepts from different courses cross-fertilize one another creating a shared discourse across the curriculum; students connect course content to their lived experience as they converse together at community dinners, praxis reflections, or bus rides home. Throughout all of this, students find a network of support to assist them as they process the difficult Salvadoran reality they encounter each day.

I recall once visiting a group of students the semester after they returned home from the *Casa*. We were discussing the challenges they faced in making the transition back to regular college life. When I asked what they missed most about El Salvador, one student replied, "the academic intensity." Immediately several others agreed. I was surprised by the response, for it is not something one typically hears about a study-abroad semester, so I asked them to explain. They all agreed on the answer. They missed the way that every part of their day had seemed focused on an integrated attempt to make sense of things that really mattered. As one student put it:

> At school I take courses, but they don't necessarily connect with one another, much less with what is happening with my friends, my life, or the place where I volunteer. And my friends are going in a thousand different directions as well. Life here seems fragmented. It was different at the *Casa*. There we were living together, struggling through the same types of praxis experiences, sharing the same courses, processing it each night in community, applying it to our lives.

In many ways, this type of integrated learning environment hearkens back to the old ideal of the Jesuit residential college, and knowing this type of environment exists is a tremendous asset in designing a course. One can think beyond what will happen within the four walls of the classroom and take advantage of the learning that naturally occurs in every aspect of the students' day. As discussed above, the most important connection to reinforce is the link between academic reflection and praxis. However, the integration of the *Casa* program prompts instructors to seek out other synergies as well. For example, midway through the semester the students have a three-day Ignatian retreat. This provides an excellent venue to let students appropriate the course material in a more personal way by incorporating it into retreat reflections and worship. Further synergies can be found by drawing on other courses in the *Casa* curriculum. For instance, toward the end of the semester, I invite students to synthesize their praxis experience by integrating final projects from other courses (such as digital storytelling from their praxis seminar or creative art from their liberation theology course) into the final synthesis paper for my class.

A different way to leverage the *Casa*'s holistic learning environment is to design coursework so that it intentionally promotes informal, philosophical conversations outside of class. Toward this end, we have movie nights and evenings of philosophical storytelling where students can explore concepts from class in informal settings. Another tool to foster dialogue outside of class is a one-page essay that is written each week in response to a specific question about the texts and films assigned for that week. In part this assignment is given to ensure that students come prepared for class, but more important, it fosters a shared weekly rhythm that encourages people, as they prepare to write the paper, to talk about how the course material is connecting to what is taking place in their own lives. Thus, on a given evening, one could walk into one of the student houses and find people discussing Rahner's notion of grace, applying it to Sam Mendes' film *American Beauty*, and comparing this to moments where they were touched by grace in their praxis sites. A different evening might reveal students conversing about Marcel's phenomenology of hope, exploring how this can be seen in Krzysztof

Kieslowski's film *Blue,* and sharing how they might be struggling to find hope amid the suffering of El Salvador. Using readings and films that are not specifically connected to El Salvador has the advantage of letting students step back from the intensity of their own experience, see how theological concepts can be developed in a different context, and then freely apply these concepts to the Salvadoran reality, without feeling predisposed to do this in a particular way by the texts themselves.

Recollection and Pedagogical Accompaniment

In imagining how course material will facilitate student transformation, I have found it useful to think of the class texts working in conjunction with three other "exterior texts": the students' praxis experiences, their shared community life in the *Casa,* and their prior history (especially the history of their own brokenness that is being called forth by the suffering they encounter in their praxis sites). Real transformation happens when students can begin to connect these "texts," and see how they jointly are inviting them to new ways of understanding themselves and the world. To borrow Parker Palmer's words, they begin to "let their life speak" and to listen to the "life that wants to live in them."[11] In these moments, not only does the course material take on a fuller meaning, but more important, students move beyond a mere intellectual appropriation of the course concepts. They begin to see how their experiences resonate with the theology and philosophy they are studying, and how together these are calling them to new faith commitments and new ways of serving those most in need. In this sense, the movement is a vocational one—helping students to open their eyes and hearts in order to discern where God is drawing them.

Crucial to this process is the example of the Salvadoran people. Their willingness to open their hearts and readily to share even the most difficult moments of their past encourages a similar openness in the *Casa* community. Their faith that God is at work even in the darkest moments inspires a similar trust. Together this combination of vulnerability and hope invites students to reflect on their lives in new ways and to risk sharing them as never before.

A concept that is particularly helpful in explaining this process of reflection to students is Gabriel Marcel's notion of "recollection":

---

11. See Parker J. Palmer, *Let Your Life Speak: Listening to the Voice of Vocation* (San Francisco: Jossey-Bass, 2000) 3–4.

The word means what it says—the act whereby I re-collect myself as a unity; but this hold, this grasp upon myself, is also relaxation and abandon. *Abandon to . . . relaxation in the presence of . . .*

It is within recollection that I take up my position—or rather, I become capable of taking up my position—in regard to my life; I withdraw from it in a certain way, but not as the pure subject of cognition; *in this withdrawal I carry with me that which I am and which perhaps my life is not.* This brings out the gap between my being and my life. . . .

I would say here that we come up against the paradox of that actual mystery whereby the I into which I withdraw ceases, for as much, to belong to itself. "You are not your own"—this great saying of St. Paul assumes in this connection its full and concrete ontological significance.[12]

Marcel's account of recollection inspires students to step back from a task-oriented view of their life and to focus instead on gathering together those moments and parts of themselves that, taken as a whole, afford a glimpse into a deeper sense of being.

One-on-one conversations are extremely important in the process of recollection. In a way analogous to spiritual direction or spiritual accompaniment, these conversations provide a space for people to attend to the inner movements of their lives. Unlike spiritual accompaniment (which explicitly focuses on such interior movements to discern how God is at work in one's world), these conversations focus more on the course material, and use it to help students articulate how they are being impacted by their praxis sites and challenged to grow. In this sense, the conversations can be seen as a kind of "pedagogical accompaniment." Such accompaniment seeks to create a safe space where students can identify a pattern emerging through significant moments in their lives, revisit those moments that continue to hold them bound, and ultimately reintegrate them into a new narrative that reflects their emerging sense of God, self, and vocation. Frequently aspects of the narratives that are tried out in these private conversations are later shared in more public settings such as classroom presentations or telling "life stories" at community nights, and this helps to solidify the students' transformation.

To encourage the formation of these transformative narratives, I ask the students to write a final paper that analyzes their experience through the lens of the philosophical framework that has been developed in class. This final paper promotes a key goal of the pedagogical accompaniment: to enable students to recollect their history and discern how the experience in El Salvador has not only affected them but also called them to new ways of being.

12. Gabriel Marcel, "On the Ontological Mystery," in *The Philosophy of Existentialism* (New York: Citadel Press, 1964) 23–24.

To illustrate the types of narratives that emerge through pedagogical accompaniment, let me share parts of one final paper from a student whom I will call Anne.

When Anne arrived at the *Casa*, life's disappointments and a sharply critical mind had made her skeptical of the "easy answers" offered by her childhood faith. Though doubtful that any answers could be found, she was still searching for some sense of God, or meaning, in which she could believe. She struggled for much of the semester not only with health issues but also with how to understand the love and suffering she encountered at her praxis site. It was only toward the end of her time that she began to look back and "re-collect" a pattern that had been emerging all along:

> The events happened slowly, almost gently, and it took months for me to realize what was happening. It was as though life—reality—was a lover, patient and persistent, waiting until I finally had to give in. I had no control over my body, and spent many days being sick; I had no control over the love that people kept freely giving me, and had to accept it, undeserved; I had no control over the children at my praxis site, and had to accept the fact that they were never going to listen to me; I had no control over other people's lives, and could not save Gloria Santos. I eventually had to concede to the fact, colossal and horrifying, that I was not actually in control of my own life.

As happens so often, Anne's own transformation flowed out of the friendships she formed with the people in her praxis site. One family in particular touched her:

> Gloria Santos is thirty years old, and she has HIV. Her husband died of AIDS a few years ago, and she is the single mother of four children. She has three sons, Mario, Carlos, and Jose; they're in the after school program at Centro Hogar, where I teach English. One Wednesday afternoon, looking through Jose's file, I chanced upon a letter that Gloria had written to Centro Hogar. The note was written with pencil on torn and dirtied loose-leaf paper in a shaky hand. It was fraught with misspellings and grammatical errors, and looked as though a first grader had written it. The letter spoke of her inability to pay for electricity bills and water bills and her difficulty in affording to feed her children. It lamented the fact that there would not be enough money to pay for this month's tuition, or for last month's. I held this letter in my hands, reading it over and over again. It broke my heart. Parents were supposed to solve problems; they were supposed to hand in notes on pretty stationery with a sure and practiced hand. The notes that children took with them to school were supposed to speak of having to leave early for doctors appointments or for family vacations—how could

it be that this woman, this mother, was writing to tell the school that she could not afford to pay for tuition?

Anne knew Mario, Carlos, and Jose well, and the shock of reading this note moved her to want to meet their mother. She went to visit Gloria at home. There they talked of her health, her financial problems, her struggle to raise four children after recently losing her job. Then one afternoon Gloria showed Anne the family photo album:

> Together, we looked through all of her pictures—we laughed and smiled at photos of her wedding, and her children's baptisms and birthday parties—and when we got to a picture of her husband, she ran her finger over it slowly. She told me that he had lost a lot of weight in the months before he died; that near the end, she could barely recognize him he was so thin. I looked at Gloria, with her skinny little arms and legs, and noticed for the first time how absolutely skeletal she was. She was silent for a while, just rubbing her bony knees while tears rolled down her face, and then she looked at me directly in the eyes, her gaze so strong and unwavering that it caught me off guard. She asked me how God could have permitted this to happen. And I had no response. I just held her while she cried, running my hands through her thin black hair, wishing with my entire being that I could cure her, that I could give her the money to pay her bills, that I could do anything besides sit in her wretched apartment and cry.

Not surprisingly that moment continued to haunt Anne. In class we were studying Jerome Miller's *The Way of Suffering*. As she reflected on her response to Gloria in light of Miller's phenomenology of crisis, she began to see her semester in a new light:

> That afternoon in the apartment fleshed out for me what Jerome Miller meant by tragic reversal. Miller writes, ''the only alternative to being devastated is the will to be in control,''[13] and for years, I had chosen the latter. Somehow, though, that afternoon, I found that I was no longer able to fit this woman and her struggles into the small, controllable world I had created. I had encountered something that challenged my entire way of being in the world. Here was this dying woman, sobbing in my arms, telling me how horrified she was of death and of not being able to take care of her children in the way that she would like to—and I found myself completely helpless, powerless to do anything but sit and hold her while

---

13. Jerome Miller, *The Way of Suffering: A Geography of Crisis* (Washington, DC: Georgetown University Press, 1988) 47. Anne is referring to Miller's idea that the attempt to avoid things in our lives unwittingly sets up a dynamic that leads to a moment of crisis in which we are invited to let the "small, controllable" world created by these avoidances be called into question by the larger reality that we have unknowingly called down upon ourselves.

she cried. Here was something that I could not, in any way, control. Despite every desire to the contrary, there was no way on earth that I could save Gloria Santos. . . .

The things I had spent so much time fastidiously controlling—my weight, my grades, my relationships, my reactions—paled. And not only paled, but became absolutely diminutive—flagrantly absurd—like an army general who spends all of his time meticulously cleaning his accordion while his troops are dying on the battlefield. . . .

I was broken apart and left cracked open by the very "things I had spent my whole life trying to avoid."[14] I would have had God come to me while I was attempting to pray, or quite conceivably through a book or through a loving Salvadoran—though no one, of course, so absolutely devastating as Gloria—but the divine could never have been made present to me through those types of experiences, all of them fitting into the mold that I had created. There was no way that God, this Infinite, could have been made present in my life without destroying my tiny, incorrect picture. "What makes life so horrible," says a priest from *The Shrine at Altamira*, "is that our salvation never comes in the form we would have chosen."[15]

In the rest of the paper, Anne discussed what followed from this moment with Gloria and how she had come to realize that her "tiny, incorrect picture"— her previous images of faith—were too small to make sense of the God she was encountering amid the suffering of El Salvador. As she moved to a more expansive theology, she was able to see her own life and her call to accompany those in need in different and more life-giving ways. The constraints of this essay prevent us from detailing all the ways Anne changed; however, I would like to touch on one change that is emblematic of a shift in perspective students often experience as they accompany the poor. Anne wrote:

William Lynch says in "Theology and Imagination" that "We have a very great fear of the finite and the human condition; we are scandalized precisely by the limitations of man . . ."[16] I felt acutely that fear of my own finitude, and of the human condition in which I found myself. I had held for so long the Gnostic imagination; I could not place trust in the finite, because I realized that I could not control it. Yet, even in the midst of the fear and hatred I felt towards these limitations and imperfections, I had the sense that I could find truth in them. Saint Paul said, "I glory in my infirmities." This, I think is the crux of it—*finding God in the last place I would have looked, in the middle of all the things about myself and the world I hated most, the things that I could not control.*

14. See Miller, *The Way of Suffering*, 61.
15. John L'Heureux, *The Shrine at Altamira* (New York: Grove Press, 1992) 238.
16. William F. Lynch, "Theology and the Imagination," *Thought* 29 (Spring 1954) 67.

Formation of a Christic Imagination

Anne's comment speaks to fundamental questions that naturally arise for students at the *Casa*: What attitude do we take toward the inevitable experience of limitation and suffering in human life? To be human is to be finite, to be incomplete, to have a sense of not having, or being, all that we might want. How do we deal with these limits? What stance do we take toward our own powerlessness? William Lynch writes:

> My own attitude toward these images of limitation . . . is that [they] are in themselves the path to whatever the self is seeking: to insight, or beauty, or, for that matter to God. This path is both narrow and direct: it leads, I believe, straight through our human realities, through our labor, our disappointments, our friends, our game legs, our harvests, our subjection to time. There are no shortcuts to beauty or to insight. We must *go through* the finite, the limited, the definite, omitting none of it lest we omit some of the potencies of being-in-the-flesh. . . . We waste our time if we try to go around or above or under the definite; we must literally go through it.[17]

Lynch says we must embrace reality and see the finite as a path to go through, not escape from. He calls this a "Christic" imagination because it flows from the example of Christ's kenosis in the incarnation. God saves us not by fleeing human reality but by entering into it, by embracing human finitude and limitation—even to the point of death. And the promise is that this leads, against all odds, to new life.

The contrasting imagination essentially takes an attitude that tries to reject or flee the human condition. It seeks shortcuts, a "way out," not a "way through" problems and constraints. It says "no," or more often, "yes, but . . ." to the finite reality that characterizes human existence. Lynch calls this a "Gnostic" or "Manichaean" imagination:

> Under this [term] let us first understand every attitude which contemns the finite, the limited and human levels of reality. . . .
>
> We have a very great fear of the finite and the human condition; we are scandalized precisely by the limitations of man, and our terrible insecurity only intensifies the drive toward some kind of angelism, and toward many forms of a magical release from the human, though these forms are more sophisticated and more disguised in our day than in others. We have lost a sense of wallowing around in the human. . . . We are indeed alienated

---

17. William F. Lynch, *Christ and Apollo: The Dimensions of the Literary Imagination* (New York: Sheed and Ward, 1960) 7.

from ourselves and no longer have a great theological confidence in the capacity of the finite to lead to any of the infinities we seek.[18]

More would need to be said, of course, to develop fully the difference between these two imaginations. Yet, hopefully this will suffice, for our purposes, to clarify the shift in perspective that Anne discussed in her paper. As she moved to a more Christic imagination, she began to find "God in the last place [she] would have looked"—in the midst of the human reality and suffering she had spent her whole life trying to avoid.

A similar shift frequently occurs as students move through their praxis experience. In fact, I would contend that at the heart of Kolvenbach's call for praxis-based learning is a Christic imagination that believes we must "go through the finite" and trust it to lead us to the truth, insight, and wisdom we are seeking. This might sound like an obvious, and perhaps useful, pedagogical perspective. Yet we need to realize it is not one that our students will naturally share. More often than not, I believe, they initially approach the "gritty reality" in their praxis sites with an imagination that is far more Gnostic than Christian. As educators we need to be aware of this dynamic, especially as it manifests itself in the resistance and frustrations that many students encounter as they enter into the "direct contact" we hope will transform them. What might initially seem like a failed educational experience can actually be the beginnings of a movement to a quite different way of being in the world. Think, for example, of the way Anne's encounter with Gloria began with confusion and helplessness but ultimately led to a new understanding of accompaniment and a deeper sense of faith. The story of Betty brings out another factor that frequently facilitates this type of movement.

Betty had come to El Salvador questioning much of her faith, and midway through the semester she found herself "stuck in despair." As she entered more fully into the lives of her praxis community, she found herself overwhelmed by their day-to-day struggle. She wrote, "I couldn't help but feel that any hope that I felt would be false and disrespectful of the harsh reality I was encountering all around me." Her attitude began to shift when she went with some Salvadoran friends to visit a refugee camp in Honduras where they had grown up and their family members had died:

> We walked three hours through unkempt forest. There were no trails. There was no easy way to walk through the old refugee camps; there was no shortcut to beauty. . . . It would be inadequate to simply move the graves to Salvadoran land, or to say the prayers at home: "we waste our

18. Lynch, "Theology and the Imagination," 66–68.

time if try to go around or above the definite, we must literally go through it."[19] We got lost; we found our way again past broken *pilas*, the old hospital, past gardens long overgrown and barely recognizable. What kind of hope did it take for these people to risk their lives for one another during the war? It takes a very special kind of Christic imagination that knows that the way up and out of poverty is the way down first through dying for your people. This is the kind of hope that celebrates the Eucharist in a cemetery.

We celebrated mass, literally standing over the martyred dead bodies, reaching toward the infinite in the most finite place on earth, the dead. Only a Christian would celebrate life in a cemetery, recognizing that "Christ moved down into all the realities of man to get to his father."[20] For the first time in my life and my experience in El Salvador, I felt I found the love and resurrection of Day Three. The energy I felt in Morazán was not simply love poured out, but love betrayed and regained. This is the mystery of the resurrection. For the first time, I understood the hope in the song, "*y que venga la alegría para lavar el sufrimiento*." The happiness comes in a subjunctive verb, showing that the happiness is hoped [for] not presumed, and it washes yet does not erase the suffering.

Betty's experience illustrates how the faith of the Salvadorans can play a key role in assisting students to imagine their own faith in a more Christic way. When the Salvadorans speak about the "hope of the martyrs," and show through their lives how God can still be found amid great suffering, students are challenged to think again about their own religious preconceptions. As Betty wrote: "After the trip to the refugee camp, I saw Morazán, my friends, and even myself differently. Nothing changed except my imagination, but it was the most radical thing that could have changed. I look on every experience here differently, and point towards the future with a different vision."

I have come to realize that if the course I teach is to be transformative, it must do more than provide students with an excellent understanding of certain philosophical or theological concepts. It must also help them form new imaginations. A crucial part of this process is developing a Christic approach to the finite that inspires them to more fully engage the realities they encounter in their praxis sites, especially those that involve suffering and faith.

Conclusion

One of the things I most value about teaching in El Salvador is that it forces students to make mistakes. They can't speak the language. Everything

19. Lynch, *Christ and Apollo*, 7.
20. Ibid., 13.

in the culture is confusing. They are stripped of all the tools they have developed to navigate the world. This experience of helplessness contrasts sharply with the culture of perfection and performance that tends to dominate our classroom culture. Annie Dillard writes:

> An infant who has just learned to hold his head up has a frank and forthright way of gazing about him in bewilderment. He hasn't the faintest clue where he is, and he aims to learn. In a couple of years, what he will have learned instead is how to fake it: he'll have the cocksure air of a squatter who has come to feel he owns the place.[21]

By the time our students reach their sophomore year, most of them have become "cocksure squatters," and in many ways our educational system rewards such mastery. Yet there can be something tremendously valuable when the limits of this secure world get shattered. One of the great benefits of direct contact with "gritty reality" is that it opens students to such moments. As in the cases of Anne and Betty, most people who come to the *Casa* experience a movement from mastery to mystery. They cannot secure and manage life as they previously had hoped, and this leaves them undefended, and open to experiences of transcendence and wonder. To quote again from Annie Dillard:

> In making the thick darkness a swaddling band for the sea, God "set bars and doors" and said, "Hitherto shalt thou come, but no further." But have we come even that far? Have we rowed out to the thick darkness, or are we all playing pinochle in the bottom of the boat?[22]

It is a wonderful image: a tiny boat rowing on a vast sea toward an endless horizon. Praxis-based learning regularly leads students to such moments of awe. Accompanying the "disadvantaged and oppressed" encourages students to stop "playing pinochle in the bottom of the boat" and to realize that they are in a world far vaster, and more complex, than they might ever have imagined. In this essay, I have tried to suggest that Father Kolvenbach's insistence on praxis-based learning makes sense not merely because it is the good or right thing to do but because it is an academically excellent way to transform lives. When intellectual analysis is rooted in the lives of those who suffer most, minds and hearts are changed. When, at last, we dare to stick our heads up from the bottom of the boat, and embrace this reality in all its concrete finitude and limitation, we paradoxically find wonder, awe, and, at times, even God.

21. Annie Dillard, *The Annie Dillard Reader* (New York: HarperCollins, 1994) 290.
22. Ibid., 286.

——————— *Chapter 9* ———————

Immersion Trips

Stephen J. Pope

Pope John Paul II maintained that every Catholic institution of higher learning must have "an institutional commitment to the service of the people of God and of the human family." This service, he insisted, should lead academic communities to be particularly attentive to the "poorest and to those who suffer economic, social, cultural, or religious injustice."[1] Immersion trips to the developing world provide one way of cultivating this kind of attention. This chapter will focus on an eight-day immersion trip to El Salvador developed by the campus ministry program at Boston College. Immersion trips intend to help students become more aware of the challenges facing marginalized communities and their residents.

We can begin by noting four important points regarding immersion trips. First, they proceed on the belief that person-to-person communication can be a special stimulus to learning and personal growth, and, as John Paul II understood, that solidarity is best learned not only through "concepts" but also through "contact."[2] Many college students, for example, are familiar with the fact that 40 percent of the world's population lives on less than two dollars per day[3] but most have not actually heard poor people themselves tell their stories. Immersion trips devote the bulk of their time to meetings, conversations, and group activities in order to facilitate listening, communication, and understanding.

1. John Paul II, *Ex corde ecclesiae*, nos. 13, 40.
2. See John Paul II, Address to Catholic University of the Sacred Heart, Milan, May 5, 2000, n. 9., cited in Rev. Peter-Hans Kolvenbach, S.J., "The Service of Faith and the Promotion of Justice in American Higher Education," at http://www.scu.edu/news/ attachments/ kolvenbach_speech.html, accessed March 19, 2009, III.A, n. 24.
3. See World Development Report 2008, at http://web.worldbank.org, accessed April 10, 2009.

Second, immersion trips help students encounter the other to provoke significant personal transformation. As Gustavo Gutierrez observes, "Rediscovering the other means entering his own world. It also means a break with ours. The world of inward-looking absorption with self . . . is not only interior but is socio-culturally conditioned. To enter the world of the other . . . with the actual demands involved . . . is to begin . . . a process of conversion."[4] Physical travel allows one to encounter the social, moral, and spiritual world of the other. Unsettling experience provokes a very different way of thinking about the world and one's place in it. The brevity of these trips, of course, would make it an exaggeration to claim that they create new friendships between our students and their hosts, but they can reasonably be said to provide space for the creation of meaningful, though temporary, connections that can in turn lead to deeper habits of solidarity in our students.

Third, personal encounters with people struggling with poverty and other forms of marginalization play a particularly important role in education for faith and justice. Catholic higher education is for the whole person—body, mind, and spirit. If we are to avoid producing "educated Eichmanns," we have to be committed to developing our students' moral sensitivity and sense of social responsibility.[5] An experience of global injustice can provide an important basis for coming to a greater understanding of it.

The experience of El Salvador is case in point. Some students find their experience in El Salvador to reinforce what they have already learned intellectually about faith and justice, but others (and these are more numerous) are shaken and disturbed by what, for them, is a first close contact with serious and widespread human deprivation. This encounter presents a dramatic and even radical challenge to the students' previous self-understanding and way of life. Students can be shocked at the violence people have had to endure, the way in which human lives are treated as worthless, and the loneliness and pain undergone by families that are geographically fragmented by economic necessity. Students are disturbed not only at massive inequality that divides the rich and poor but even more by the fact that El Salvador is symptomatic of the entire global order.

Fourth, immersion trips facilitate encounters with the poor in and through community. Rather than a set of parallel individual journeys or a collection of people engaged in a silent retreat, immersion trips constitute an ongoing experience of community in which friends grow together in their understand-

---

4. Gustavo Gutierrez, "Liberation, Theology and Proclamation," in *Theology of Liberation, Concilium* 6/10, ed. Claude Geffré and Gustavo Gutierrez (June 1974) 59.

5. Kolvenbach, "The Service of Faith and the Promotion of Justice in American Higher Education."

ing of themselves, one another, and those with whom they interact. Personal transformation is facilitated through building trust, communication, and mutual care within the group.

Journeying to a distant location can build community among students in a unique way. The stress of travel, geographical dislocation, cultural awkwardness, loneliness, and sometimes even physical illness are uncomfortable, but they can also facilitate deeper friendships. Getting out of the usual campus "bubble" enables participants to view one another and their place in the world differently, but it only works if each member of the team feels appreciated and respected, if each learns to cooperate with others, and if student leaders encourage multifaceted participatory teamwork. Perhaps most important, ongoing group reflection and prayer allows for more authentic modes of mutual self-disclosure, sharing, and empathic understanding than occurs in everyday campus life. Friendship within the group gives students the space for sharing their struggles and for asking difficult questions about what they see and hear in the other country; it also provides much-needed support after returning to campus to friends who are oblivious or indifferent.

The danger of tight community among student participants is twofold. One temptation lies in conformity to "group think" in which individual students can feel pressure to conform to what other students feel about various experiences. To protect against this temptation, it is important that students be allowed to ask critical questions such as "Is CAFTA really that bad?" "Didn't the U.S. need to fight communism in Central America?" or "What right do Salvadorans have to come to the U.S. and take jobs away from American workers?" The danger here is that the real learning and intellectual transformation that happens when students freely broach and wrestle with uncomfortable questions can be short-circuited by self-censorship based on perceptions of "political correctness."[6]

A second temptation lies in exclusivity. Students returning from immersion trips often experience a disconnection with their old friends at home and on campus. Friends share a bond and give support to another but can seem to outsiders to be a social justice clique that makes others feel excluded, diminished in value, and judged negatively. Students faced with this possibility thus have to be careful to show respect for, hospitality to, and appreciation for their other friends.

6. See George Orwell, "Politics and the English Language," at http://orwell.ru/library/essays/politics/english/e_polit, accessed April 12, 2009. Originally published in *Horizon*, London, 1946.

Why Spend Money to Visit Poor People in Another Country?

At this point we can return to the question about immersion trips noted above: why spend money to visit poor people in another country? At least two claims are implied in this criticism.

First, there is no need to travel far away when we have poor people in our own cities. It is of course true that poverty in the United States is debilitating, degrading, and harmful, to the poor. As physician Paul Farmer notes, "deprived groups in the 'First World' live, in many ways, in the 'Third.'" African Americans in some major cities, he points out, have a "lower life expectancy at birth than do most people in immensely poorer China or even India."[7] Many migrant agricultural workers in Florida, to note another example, suffer as much as their counterparts in Latin America.[8]

Yet this objection misses the fact that this travel enables students to understand features of global poverty that can more easily be missed by those whose attention is focused exclusively on local communities. One can see in El Salvador, for example, the negative effects of U.S. immigration policy, U.S. military aid, and U.S. markets and monetary policy on ordinary Salvadorans.

The conditions of the poor of El Salvador are significantly different from those of the United States. Economist Branko Milanovic of the World Bank points out: "An American having the average income of the bottom US decile is better-off than 2/3 of world population."[9] El Salvador lies in the mid-range among countries in the world, somewhere between Timor-Leste (with a Gross National Income at Purchasing Power Parity per capita income of $400) and Luxembourg (with a GNI PPP per capita income of $66,000).[10] The rural poor of El Salvador lack indoor plumbing, safe drinking water, and realistic access to even minimal secondary education, and the urban poor face the highest levels of violent crime among nations not at war.

Firsthand exposure to poverty in El Salvador usually has a powerful effect even on students who have had considerable experience in service in the

---

7. Paul Farmer, *Pathologies of Power: Health, Human Rights, and the New War on the Poor* (Berkeley: University of California Press, 2005) xii.

8. See Breanne Gilpatrick, "Farm Workers from Immokalee Protest," *Miami Herald*, March 10, 2009, at http://www.miamiherald.com/news/florida/ story/ 941301.html, accessed March 19, 2009. See also the Coalition of Immokalee Workers: http://www.ciw-online.org/, accessed March 19, 2009.

9. Branko Milanovic, "True World Income Distribution, 1988 and 1993: First Calculation Based on Household Surveys Alone," *The Economic Journal* 112/476 (January 2002) 51–92, at 89. See also Larry Elliott and Charlotte Denny, "Top 1% Earn as Much as the Poorest 56%," *The Guardian*, Friday, January 18, 2002.

10. See http://www.nationsonline.org/oneworld/GNI_PPP_of_countries.htm, accessed March 12, 2009.

United States. Listening to a local human rights activist say that eight people are killed in her neighborhood each day helps students understand the vulnerability of the poor in a new way, to see what it means not to have an effective police force or a fair criminal justice system, and to grasp the dim prospects for virtually unemployable young adults. Seeing these evils in such graphic and extreme ways can prod our students to become more sensitive to social evils that exist on the streets of our own cities.

The visit to the notorious massacre site of El Mozote illustrates the potential impact of this kind of travel. It is one thing to read about the attack of December 1981 that involved the murder of 767 innocent men, women, and children, and another to stand on that sacred ground and listen to the daughter of the sole survivor describe its impact on people of that area. Students are not quite the same once they have seen the El Mozote rose garden over the site of a chapel in which over 131 children under the age of 12 were shot, stabbed, or burned alive.[11] It is hard not to be shaken, moreover, by the fact that some of the officers who commanded these troops were American trained, transported in American-made vehicles, and used American weapons and ammunition. El Mozote always provokes questions from students on a range of issues from the ethics of American foreign policy during the Reagan years and the utility of the just war doctrine to theological questions about theodicy, sin, and forgiveness.

A second dimension of the criticism of immersion trips insists that it is more important to help poor people than to visit them. This specific criticism concedes the pedagogical value of the trips to college students but argues that the preferential option gives priority to service of the poor over the education of the rich. In response we might note that service trips run the danger of reinforcing the widespread paternalistic assumption that college volunteers are using their supposedly superior talents to help feckless natives. Any trip that reinforces arrogance, of course, is counterproductive.

While it is true that one week of service will never make a tangible and lasting impact on one's host community, it is also the case that it can have a part to play in a process of personal transformation. The intent of immersion trips is thus not simply to have students "visit" poor communities but rather to provide them with an opportunity to better understand marginalized communities.

11. See United Nations Truth Commission Report, *From Madness to Hope*, IV.C.1: Illustrative Case: El Mozote, at http://www.usip.org/library/tc/doc/reports/el _salvador/tc_ es_03151993_casesC.html, accessed March 20, 2009. See also Mark Danner, *The Massacre at El Mozote: A Parable of the Cold War* (New York: Vintage, 1994).

The immersion trip to El Salvador creates conditions for kinds of conversation and conversion that are most likely to happen not in the comfort of dorm rooms or campus lounges but in the communities of those from whom we most need to hear. We learn best on *their* ground and on *their* terms, and not on our own. One hopes that students who receive care and hospitality will be less likely to think of themselves as "heroes" who have come to save "nice" but, it is assumed, incompetent poor people. The transition from this paternalism to an attitude of humility, respect, and appreciation is the key to developing the virtue of solidarity.

Instead of simply "driving by" local communities, then, students have to enter them with respect, a desire to engage in conversation, and an ability to empathize with their people. The primary skills to be developed are those of active listening, paying attention, asking appropriate and thoughtful questions, and taking seriously the words and self-expression of one's hosts in such a way that the "other" is no longer regarded as "strange," "alien," or "weird."

Having said this, one might wonder if travel for the sake of understanding is not still a subtle way of merely "using" those who offer hospitality to our students. Admittedly, even the best-intentioned visitors face the constant temptation of regarding the poor as mere pedagogical instruments, especially if immersion trips involve only intense emotional experiences without intellectual engagement, meaningful personal change, or practical follow-up.[12]

This is why it is important that students returning from El Salvador engage in concrete follow-up activities. These include awareness-raising events on campus and fund-raising efforts to provide scholarships or resources to meet the expressed needs of the host community. The more serious these kinds of follow-up efforts, the less self-referential the immersion trip is likely to be.

The danger of "poverty tourism" is never completely eliminated.[13] Campus fund-raising is valuable but a "drop in the bucket" when it comes to the thirst for justice of the poor of El Salvador. Mature students, however, recognize that a little water is better than none, and they come to learn that they have gained more from their hosts than they can give back. The experience of gratitude inspires the realization that those who have been "takers" in the past now need to learn how both to give and to receive in a spirit of solidarity.

---

12. For an excellent discussion of solidarity, see Albert Nolan, O.P., "Spiritual Growth and the Option for the Poor," at http://www.laymission-comboni.org/images/nolanpdf.pdf, accessed August 18, 2009.

13. See Jo Ann van Engen, "The Cost of Short-term Missions," *The Other Side* 36 (January 2000) 3.

Immersion trips may have their most important role in helping students to think more seriously about how to make solidarity an important part of their adult lives. Just as a person does not become physically fit after one week in the gym, so students do not become paragons of solidarity after one immersion trip. Yet the powerful insights students can gain from such a trip can play an important role in shaping their deepest ideals and commitments over a lifetime. Their professional energies might not be directed to El Salvador in particular, but they can infuse solidarity into how they work in their careers, how they raise their children, and how they function as citizens and as members of civil society. It can inspire them to be much more alert to wider issues of structural injustice in areas such as immigration law, trade agreements, and environmental policies, and perhaps even lead some to work with organizations dedicated to addressing large-scale social problems.

Levels of Personal Transformation

The preceding reflections can be complemented with a brief analysis of the kind of personal transformation that immersion trips strive to affect. Catholic universities are different from many other institutions of higher learning in that they explicitly profess to be dedicated to the formation of the whole person—affective as well as cognitive; religious, moral, and social as well as intellectual. Dean Brackley, professor at El Salvador's University of Central America, points out that our universities ought not only to prepare our students to come to a more adequate understanding of the world but also enable them "to change the world when they leave the university."[14] Yet before our students want to change the world, they must want to change themselves. Immersion trips promote this change on at least three levels: social, moral, and spiritual, and each of these levels has both emotional and intellectual dimensions.

Social Transformation

Social transformation involves the gradual awakening of mind and heart to the realities of global injustice and to a corresponding sense of social responsibility. If they had been born as an average person in El Salvador, our students would most likely not have attended college, since Salvadorans have on average only 6 years of formal education. They would probably also

---

14. Dean Brackley, S.J., "Higher Standards for Higher Education: The Christian University and Solidarity," at http://www.creighton.edu/CollaborativeMinistry/brackley.html, accessed June 4, 2006.

have family members dislocated to North America (where 3 million of a total population of 10 million Salvadorans live). They would earn the per capita income estimated by the IMF to be approximately $3,000, in contrast to the U.S. per capita income of approximately $47,000. If their social location were determined by lottery, they would (like the global population) have nearly a 4 in 10 chance of living in poverty[15] and a 20 percent chance of living in absolute poverty (i.e., forced to live on less than $1 a day).[16] If our students were Salvadoran, they would probably live with what the UN World Food Program calls "vulnerability to food and nutritional insecurity," a problem that has been exacerbated by the global rise in food prices during the last two years.[17] They would not be casually spending $5 on a tall coffee latte and muffin at Starbucks. They would also be subject not only to the street violence noted above but also to a relatively high degree of vulnerability to natural disasters, including earthquakes, droughts, landslides, hurricanes, floods, and volcanic eruptions.

These facts can be easily gleaned from the internet without the inconvenience and expense of international travel. Yet, as noted above, face-to-face encounters help to show the human significance of what is studied in the classroom or read about in the library. Such encounters help students to recognize the challenges that Salvadorans have to face on a daily basis: searching for work, trying to help one's children get an education, avoiding street crime or dealing with its effects, dealing with the indignity of prejudice and discrimination, coping with an inability to obtain justice from the criminal justice system, and facing the dehumanizing consequences of domestic abuse.

15. From 2006–07 poverty rose from 30.7 to 34.6 percent of the total population. See UN, World Food Program: Country Report: El Salvador, at http://www.wfp.org/countries/el-salvador, accessed March 9, 2009.

16. The meaning of "poverty" of course can be determined in a variety of ways. The UN Copenhagen Declaration describes poverty as "a condition characterized by severe deprivation of basic human needs, including food, safe drinking water, sanitation facilities, health, shelter, education and information." (See the World Summit for Social Development Programme of Action, "Eradication of Poverty," chap. 2, par. 19, at http://www.un-documents.net/poa-wssd .htm#chapter-2, accessed March 9, 2009.) The "poverty line" is ordinarily said to be the line of income beneath which one does not have the financial resources with which to purchase the goods necessary for living. The World Bank determines this poverty line to be $1 a day for the least developed countries (most of which are in Africa) and $2 for middle income economies such as those in Latin America. The poverty line is calculated in terms of "purchasing power parity" that takes into account the differences between the costs of living in different national contexts. Recent development of a "capabilities approach" to poverty takes into account not only income but also other factors essential for human well-being.

17. See UN, World Food Program: Country Report: El Salvador, at http://www.wfp. org/countries/el-salvador, accessed March 9, 2009.

An enlarged understanding of the nature of our society and its place in the world leads to questions about its justice and about what we ought to do about it. As John Paul II wrote in his apostolic exhortation *Ecclesia in America*, true conversion seeks continuously to bridge "the gap between faith and life" and moves us toward "solidarity, because it makes us aware that whatever we do for others, especially for the poorest, we do for Christ himself."[18] A growing awareness of the radical disparities of life opportunities that separates our students from their Salvadoran counterparts leads them to raise questions about local and global distributive justice: Why does one relatively small group of people in El Salvador manage to monopolize so much of a country's income and wealth while a vast number of others are deprived of the basics? Why is the deck so strongly stacked against the poor? These kinds of questions naturally give rise to a set of questions pertaining to our own country: Is it right that average citizens of the United States have greater life opportunities than do Salvadorans? How do we understand the wealth disparities in our own country?

Participation in immersion trips helps students come to a better understanding of their *own* lives in relation to those of their peers in El Salvador. Students have had to work diligently in high school to be admitted to Boston College, but the Salvadoran experience helps them understand that they themselves did not create the social conditions that allow their hard work to be supported and credited so richly. We all know abstractly that we do not deserve being born of one particular set of parents in one culture rather than in another, yet we in the United States often do not fully appreciate the implications of this fact for our own life chances and its negative implication for many Salvadorans. Thus students often come to understand themselves as beneficiaries of a broad set of social conditions for which neither they nor their parents can take credit.

The recognition of privilege helps to provoke questions of social responsibility. Students ask about the justice of paying $50,000 per year on a Boston College education when most young people in El Salvador, no matter how talented or hardworking, cannot even afford secondary education. Realization of their own privilege leads some students to initially feel guilty, but guilt is beside the point. Students ideally come to see privilege as bringing responsibility to serve those who do not have such opportunity. This process catalyzes their move from feeling entitled to certain goods to regarding their talents and opportunities as social assets for which they are accountable. If

---

18. John Paul II, *Eccelsia in America*, no. 26.

there is, as John Paul II put it, a "social mortgage" on private property,[19] then there is also a social mortgage on our own power.[20]

What students see in El Salvador highlights aspects of American society to which they had previously been at best only vaguely aware. The social level of transformation rejects not only the common assumption that the global distribution of burdens and benefits is, on balance, fair and just, but also recognizes the human costs of such a misconception.[21] Students often begin to see the "land of plenty" as also the "land of luxury," "conspicuous consumption," and inexcusable waste.

Undergraduates viewing a new American-style mall in San Salvador that displaced hundreds of poor Salvadoran families, who themselves could never even dream of shopping in such stores, cannot help but think about both malls and neighborhoods in new ways. A junior from Boston described her impression of one scene this way: "On either side of one highway were high-priced malls and expensive car dealerships. In the median strip between two fast lanes were families living off the last remains of coffee plants after the development, in homes I couldn't imagine existed—until I saw them."

The lessons of Salvadoran mall displacement are also relevant to similarly situated communities in our own society. Students conversing with Salvadorans about this kind of displacement come back to the United States with a new eye for how things look from the point of view of the marginalized. That they consider how different certain circumstances must appear to the poor shows an important transformation that would be nearly impossible to achieve in the classroom alone. In fact, students usually become much more attuned to the poor of our country after encountering the poor of El Salvador. Homeless people downtown who used to be "invisible," for example, now come into clear focus; those previously described as "illegals" are now seen as men and women struggling to make a living under very difficult circumstances; and the food-service workers in our cafeterias are now acknowledged to have names, hearts and minds, histories and homes. That they now count as human persons in itself constitutes a major breakthrough.

19. *Sollicitudo rei socialis*, December 30, 1987, no. 42. See also John Paul II, "Address at the Opening of the Third General Conference of the Latin-American Bishops" (January 28, 1979): *AAS* 71 (1979), pp. 189–96; Ad Limina Address to a Group of Polish Bishops (December 17, 1987), n. 6: *L'Osservatore Romano*, December 18, 1987.

20. See David Hollenbach, *The Common Good and Christian Ethics* (New York: Cambridge University Press, 2002), chap. 6 on "intellectual solidarity."

21. See Melvin J. Lerner, *The Belief in a Just World: A Fundamental Delusion* (New York: Plenum Press, 1980); and Claire Andre and Manual Velasquez, "The Just World Theory," Markkula Center for Applied Ethics, Santa Clara University, at http://www.scu.edu/ethics/publications/iie/v3n2/justworld.html, accessed April 9, 2009.

Moral Transformation

Moral transformation includes both the social concern just discussed but also a willingness to be conscientious in living one's life as a member of a community. It involves not just seeing and judging more adequately but also acting more responsibly. Immersion trips foster moral transformation most directly by inspiring a more intense dedication to social justice and more broadly by heightening one's moral awareness and sense of right and wrong, strengthening and sharpening one's conscience, and deepening one's commitment to moral goodness in general.

The purpose of immersion trips should not be reduced to the promotion of social justice, and social transformation unaccompanied by moral improvement is lopsided and stunted. Some students come to hold passionate convictions about social justice while being oblivious to the application of love and justice to their own lives, particularly when it comes to sexual behavior and the consumption of alcohol or drugs. It is sometimes easier to write a paper about immigration reform than to be fair to a classmate or truthful to a girlfriend. A commitment to social justice is only authentic if accompanied by an equal commitment to personal moral integrity.

One of the values of the Salvadoran trip concerns the way it makes apparent the injustice of patriarchy, the cultural prevalent rationalizations of sexism, and the evils of gender-based violence. The denigration of women in a machismo culture reveals in a very dramatic way the consequences of valuing women for certain traits but without acknowledging that they bear the same dignity or moral value as men. Seeing the gender injustices in El Salvador helps students to recognize those of our own society, and perhaps (especially for male students) even to see flaws that they would not have previously noticed. It highlights the need for moral conversion in gender as well as class and racial domains.

The major obstacle to this dimension of transformation lies in a popular culture that identifies human fulfillment with the acquisition of wealth, status, and pleasure, and that reduces freedom to radical autonomy. Just as compassion for the poor is mere sentimentality unless accompanied by justice and solidarity, so the latter amounts to social posturing unless accompanied by virtues of self-control and courage in one's personal life. Social justice best takes root in people who are not driven by their appetites or fears. Further, actions for justice are likely to be short-lived and easily cast aside if not rooted in personal moral commitment.

Spiritual Transformation

Finally, spiritual transformation pertains to the development of one's sense of reverence for what is sacred, an awakening or deepening of one's faith, and an expansion of one's trust in Jesus Christ and identification with the church. Instead of opposing "religion" and "spirituality," we can understand the former as intended to promote, guide, and support the latter. Students associate Pedro Arrupe with the motto of Jesuit universities as inspiring "men and women for others," but they are usually unaware of his theocentric, Christocentric, and ecclesial vision of service. We should educate, he said, "men and women who will live not for themselves but for God and his Christ—for the God-man who lived and died for all the world."[22] The biggest obstacle to students' understanding Arrupe's vision, of course, comes from the popular assumption that one can follow Christ without participating in the life of the church. One of the primary advantages presented by faith-based immersion trips can be found in the explicit and profound way that they show students the connection between discipleship and community.

Immersion trips sometimes have their greatest impact in helping students understand the Christian life as animated by faith, hope, and charity. First, students are often inspired by the faith displayed in base Christian communities and with how the liberating message of the Gospel can lead people who have been subjected to prolonged suffering to be thankful and even joyful. I am struck by how often students remark on their experience of finding Christ in the deep faith of the Salvadoran poor. Whereas many students grow up with a rather abstract and domesticated view of Jesus, base Christian communities allow students to witness the faith of the people in Jesus specifically as a person who was marginalized and attacked because he preached good news to the poor, criticized the social structures of his day for excluding the poor, and regarded care for the least of our brothers and sisters as a condition of salvation (as in Matt 25:30-46). It is easier for many students to grasp Jesus as prophet and suffering servant when praying alongside Salvadoran campesinos at the crypt of Oscar Romero than when praying in their own home parishes.

Second, students also speak of being inspired by the hope held by the poor in the face of persistent social evil and their trust in divine providence despite the hardship of their lives. The "hope of the martyrs"[23] sustains a woman whose husband and three boys were assassinated during the civil war. Hope is presented not as an expectation of a blissful afterlife but as a deeply felt trust that God is working to promote the kingdom "on earth as it is in heaven"

---

22. "Men and Women for Others," at http://onlineministries.creighton.edu/Collaborative Ministry/men-for-others.html, accessed April 8, 2009.

23. See Jon Sobrino, *Witnesses to the Kingdom: The Martyrs of El Salvador and the Crucified Peoples* (Maryknoll, NY: Orbis Books, 2003) 153 et passim. See also Stephen J. Pope, ed., *Hope and Solidarity: Jon Sobrino's Challenge to Christian Theology* (Maryknoll, NY: Orbis Books, 2008).

and in a way that heals bodies and minds as well as souls. The experience of communities of hope helps students to differentiate between religion as an opiate and religion as a force for social transformation.

Finally, students also marvel at the kind of Christian compassion displayed in base Christian communities—people who care for one another in their deep loss, accompany the poorest of the poor, defend the widow and the orphan, shelter those hunted by death squads at the risk of their own lives, share what little food they have with those who are even hungrier, risk their lives by working with teenagers in gang-infested neighborhoods, and insist that powerful perpetrators be held accountable for their crimes. Exemplars of such compassion provide a compelling witness of the power of love to withstand and overcome evil.

First-person encounters help students come to a sharper awareness of the systemic and institutional as well as personal causes of the suffering of the poor. It also leads them to see that personal acts of compassion are necessary but not sufficient for addressing widespread and structurally rooted injustices. The poor of El Salvador make it abundantly clear that charity, the love of God and love of neighbor, generates a commitment to social justice as well as compassion.[24]

Salvadorans who work in parishes, schools, and other institutions that serve the marginalized show our students how faith, hope, and charity give rise to a long-term commitment to social justice. Most instructive are the personal stories that describe how dedicated people live in solidarity and make sense of their lives despite serious deprivation, personal danger, and sacrifice. Base Christian communities show the importance of community as the basis of faith, hope, and charity, and how believers help one another to sustain their discipleship and solidarity.

Each of these three levels of transformation reinforces the others. Spiritual transformation is seriously flawed unless it is accompanied by moral and social transformation, as we can see in religiously devout but socially myopic students who reduce personal morality to following the Ten Commandments or social morality to right-to-life politics. The deepening of faith in spiritual transformation gives rise to a moral transformation in relation to oneself and one's neighbor and to a social transformation regarding one's society and the wider world. Moral and social transformation reach their culmination in spiritual transformation, but spiritual transformation generates a complementary ongoing commitment to moral and social transformation.

---

24. See Benedict XVI, *Deus caritas est*, no. 28.

Affective and Cognitive Dimensions of Personal Transformation

Personal transformation has both affective and cognitive dimensions. Students who have not traveled in the developing world can find themselves overwhelmed at the deprivation and suffering they experience in the barrios and rural villages of El Salvador. Encountering serious poverty can elicit an array of feelings that include compassion for those who suffer, outrage and resentment over injustice, and shame at one's own previous ignorance or indifference.

Emotionally powerful reactions can inspire a desire to live in a more intentional way, to change one's attitudes, and to undertake a new commitment to justice, but they fizzle out unless they become something like "raw material" for the virtues. Emotions dissipate unless wisely reflected upon, shaped, and directed. They can contribute to a change of perspective, but they do not suffice for serious personal transformation. At their best, however, emotionally charged experiences can contribute to the development of deeper affections that support solidarity.

Life-changing decisions and undertaking serious commitments do not result from purely cognitive processes; they reflect deeper affective forms of identification. One of our students, for example, decided that living in solidarity meant postponing his professional career for a year to work for Jesuit Volunteer Corps, another found it involved teaching in the inner city rather than in a suburban school, and a third determined that it meant undertaking graduate studies in public health rather than in medicine. Each of these students decided how he or she would pursue solidarity in his or her own life, but they all shared the desire to make their life choices in light of their deepened commitment to solidarity.

Powerful emotional experiences can lead to deeper knowledge of what one cares about and generate cognitive engagement with new concerns, questions, and lines of thinking. Students cannot help but be deeply moved by a conversation with a mother whose son was disappeared, or with a son who has not seen his father in two years because he had to move to California to earn a living, or with an elderly woman who suffers debilitating back pain incurred during the hardships of the civil war. These kinds of experiences are important in their own right, yet they also lead to important questions about, for example, the meaning of accountability and forgiveness, the effect of economic migration on families, and the long-term impact of armed struggle on health.

A weeklong encounter engages a cognitive dimension of personal transformation when it inspires students to think more critically, to raise pertinent questions about their experiences, and to struggle for more adequate understanding of them. Immersion trips can provide a stimulus for attempting to overcome the vast gap students perceive between the intellectual agenda of their academic curriculum and the rest of their college experience. Dorm, gym, and cafeteria too often constitute one world, and classrooms, library, and faculty offices another. The divide between these two worlds is reduced when substantive academic research can be brought to bear on what is experienced in an immersion trip.

One example will have to suffice. It has already been noted that Boston College students have opportunities to attend prayer services at various base Christian communities in San Salvador. The first such service often takes some students by surprise because it is led by women, organized around a group discussion of the biblical texts of the day on which women and men, girls and boys are all invited to comment. The congregation's discussion generates many different views of the Scripture readings, none of which is authoritative but much of which is existentially engaging. The sincerity, mutual respect, and participatory nature of this prayer service always impresses students.

San Ramon

This worship service inevitably triggers a wide range of questions by students regarding the status of this particular group and its relation to the local parish, the meaning of the priesthood in the Catholic Church, the obstacles to the ordination of women, the role of the laity in the church, the pastoral implications of liberation theology, and so forth. An experience of prayer in this small Salvadoran faith community leads students to raise important theological questions that had previously seemed remote, pedantic, and even irrelevant.

To summarize, immersion trips promote intellectual as well as affective growth, and each reinforces the other. Our most mature and generous students undertake a personal opposition to injustice and want to make a positive long-term contribution to the common good of their own communities, if not to El Salvador itself.

Conclusion

This chapter has shown how immersion trips can contribute to the mission of Catholic universities. While registering certain besetting temptations for these types of programs, it maintains that, at their best, they can affect our students both intellectually and affectively by promoting their integral social, ethical, and religious transformation. Such programs, properly developed, can inspire students to the pursuit of faith, hope, and charity in a way that gives rise to long-term commitments to social justice. They can thus lead our graduates to be "leaven in the world" whose lives reflect "a feeling of deep solidarity with the human race and its history."[25]

25. *The Basic Sixteen Documents, Vatican Council II: Constitutions, Decrees, Declarations*, gen ed., Austin Flannery, O.P. (Northport, NY: Costello Publishing Co., 1996), "Decree on the Apostolate of Lay People, *Apostolicam actuositatem*," no. 2, and Pastoral Constitution on the Church in the Modern World, *Gaudium et spes*, no. 1, respectively. Thanks to a number of friends from Boston College who read and made helpful comments on a previous draft of this chapter: Matthew Hamilton, Meg Battle, Jeremy Marks, Tom Kelly, and Kelly Garrity.

Chapter 10

Meeting the Living God

The great patristic scholar Jaroslav Pelikan is said to have remarked ironically, shortly before his death, that he feared his grandchildren might grow up without a faith to reject. As someone who had been raised in the Lutheran tradition, Professor Pelikan was well aware that faith is more than assent to the truths articulated in the church's creeds and doctrines, important as they are. Christianity is fundamentally about a person, Jesus the Lord, the crucified one who lives and is present in his body, the church. This was at the heart of Pope Benedict's address to Catholic educators at the Catholic University of America last April. He said that "every Catholic educational institution is a place to encounter the living God who in Jesus Christ reveals his transforming love and truth (cf. *Spe salvi* 4)."[1] But I am not sure that this is really clear to many young Catholics I encounter today.

I continue to be amazed by the responses of my Catholic students when I ask them in class to define what they understand "faith" to mean. Almost universally they say something like this: faith is to believe something you cannot prove, or perhaps to believe what the church teaches. Sometimes God is mentioned, but Jesus almost never. What is clear is that most young Catholics understand faith propositionally, at least on an implicit level. Faith means for them believing certain truths; it is not seen as a relationship. It is only when an occasional evangelical student in the class says something about faith as a personal relationship with Jesus, or mentions accepting Jesus as Lord and Savior, that a more personal understanding of faith surfaces.

So how do we help our young people come to that existential encounter with the person of Christ spoken of repeatedly by Pope Benedict and Pope John Paul II before him? How can we help them to encounter the divine mystery manifest in Jesus? I would like to examine first the contemporary fascination with spirituality divorced from religion. Second, I want to consider

---

1. Pope Benedict XVI, "Speech to Educators," *Origins* 37/46 (May 1, 2008) 740.

an image of God widespread today, determined far more by popular culture than by the Christian tradition. These culturally determined visions of spirituality or religion, divorced from historic Christianity, are in my opinion obstacles to a living faith today. After examining them, I will conclude by offering some brief suggestions that might lead beyond these cultural obstacles to an encounter with the living God.

Spirituality, not Religion

If contemporary Catholicism is suffering what *America* magazine describes in its review of the Pew Forum data as "an exodus of the faithful unprecedented in its history,"[2] interest in spirituality especially among the young seems to be strong, if not increasing. Yet all too often what passes for spirituality has been divorced from religion, with its implications of creed, cult, and community. Such unmediated spirituality is privatized and subjective. In his seminal work, *A Secular Age*, Charles Taylor argues that a return to the spiritual is a very widespread option in our unbelieving culture, but the spiritual he speaks of, or spirituality as it is often called today, remains within the bounds of an impersonal framework. It does not represent a return to the transcendent but remains resolutely naturalist. Meaning is entirely immanent; it comes not from beyond but from us.[3]

One of the most optimistic testimonies about the contemporary interest of young people in spirituality comes from a report of UCLA's Higher Education Research Institute, "Spirituality in Higher Education," under the direction of Alexander W. Astin. Examining data from 14,527 students attending 136 colleges and universities nationwide, surveying students as entering freshmen in the fall of 2004 and again in the late spring of 2007 at the end of their junior year, the researchers claimed that the students showed significant growth in a wide spectrum of spiritual and ethical considerations during their college years, though their attendance at religious services actually declined during those years.[4]

The UCLA researchers used a twelve-point, self-reported scale. It listed spirituality, being on a spiritual quest, equanimity, charitable involvement, compassionate self-concept, an ethic of caring, and an ecumenical worldview. They also included five indicators of student religiousness: religious

2. "Lost Sheep," *America* 198/9 (2008) 5.

3. Charles Taylor, *A Secular Age* (Cambridge, MA: Belknap Press of Harvard University Press, 2007) 364–76.

4. See "New Study: College Students Grow in Spirituality," UCLA Online December 20, 2007: http://www.today.ucla.edu/out-about/071220_students_spirituality/.

commitment, engagement, skepticism, struggle, and religious/social conservatism as further ways to assess student spirituality. Missing, however, was any real effort to survey spiritual "practices"—including ascetic discipline, bodily exercise, regular prayer or meditation, journaling, spiritual direction, or service—that as John Coleman suggests have been traditionally considered signs of a genuine spirituality.[5] The discrepancy between the optimistic charting of spiritual interest and low level of religious practice or spiritual growth may reflect more the ideological orientation of many social scientists who tend to write as though religion and spirituality are mutually exclusive. Religion is narrowly described as formal and institutional, while spirituality is seen as personal and experiential. The result is what some religious sociologists have called a "fuzzy" concept of spirituality,[6] not to mention a very subjective notion of God.

Faith without Accountability

I have long been concerned about what I hear from many students about their images of God. They claim that their understanding of God is based on their own personal experience, but in reality it seems to reflect much more the religious individualism of contemporary American culture, with its emphasis on subjective feelings and personal preferences. As one student said, "I've always believed in God as an individual communicator, and I didn't learn about him through school or church, but experiences and people." Another said "theology is the study of faith, and faith is up to the interpretation of the individual." Recently one student wrote "a lot of my friends are not Catholic or 'anything' for that matter; they 'believe what they want to believe.' They all think there is a higher power that they define by their own terms. They expect God to be there for them in their times of need, but they never go to church or pray."

Moralistic Therapeutic Deism

In *Soul Searching*, their survey of the religious and spiritual lives of U.S. teenagers, Christian Smith and Melinda Lundquist Denton make some

---

5. See John A. Coleman, "Social Science and Spirituality," *The Blackwell Companion to Christian Spirituality*, ed. Arthur Holder (Malden, MA: Basil Blackwell, 2005) 289–307.

6. See, for example, Brian Zillbauer and Kenneth Pargament et al., "Religion and Spirituality: Unfuzzying the Fuzzy," *The Journal for the Scientific Study of Religion* 36/4 (1997) 549–84; also Penny Long Marler and C. Kirk Hadaway, "'Being Religious' or 'Being Spiritual' in America: A Zero-Sum Proposition?" *The Journal for the Scientific Study of Religion* 41/2 (2002) 289–300.

interesting comments on the way young people talk about God. They note that "religious languages and vocabularies of commitment, duty, faithfulness, obedience, calling, obligation, accountability, and ties to the past are nearly completely absent" from their discourse.[7] In an attempt to summarize the subjective image of God that emerges from their research on what teenagers say about their religious faith and beliefs, they coin the term "Moralistic Therapeutic Deism," suggesting that it represents the de facto dominant religion among contemporary U.S. teenagers, and perhaps the "new mainstream American religious faith for our culturally post-Christian, individualistic, mass-consumer society."

If Moralistic Therapeutic Deism had a creed, it would look something like this:

- A God exists who created and orders the world and watches over human life on earth.
- God wants people to be good, nice, and fair to each other, as taught in the Bible and by most world religions.
- The central goal of life is to be happy and to feel good about oneself.
- God does not need to be particularly involved in one's life except when God is needed to resolve a problem.
- Good people go to heaven when they die.[8]

In a further study which unpacks the "creed" of this de facto religion, Smith makes a number of observations which seem very much to the point. First, from the perspective of this religious view or faith, being moral means not much more than being "kind, nice, pleasant, courteous, responsible, at work on improving oneself, taking care of one's health, and doing one's best to be successful." Second, what seems to be most important are the therapeutic benefits to the believer; this kind of faith is about being happy, at peace, and successful. Third, its God remains at a safe distance; it is not a God who is personally involved, except when one wants to call on him, "mostly when one has some trouble or problem or bad feeling which one wants God" to fix.[9]

The term "deism" is adopted because, like classic deism, its God functions as the distant, impersonal deity who creates and orders the world but stays far away, distant from the lives of us humans, except when we choose

---

7. Christian Smith and Melinda Lundquist Denton, *Soul Searching: The Religious and Spiritual Lives of American Teenagers* (New York: Oxford University Press, 2005) 262.

8. Ibid., 162–63.

9. Christian Smith, "Moralistic Therapeutic Deism," in *Passing on the Faith: Transforming Traditions for the Next Generation of Jews, Christians, and Muslims*, ed. James L. Heft (New York: Fordham University Press, 2006) 64.

to seek him. There is a disconnect between its God and that of historic Christianity. As Smith says:

> This is not primarily a saving God of grace and forgiveness, or a Trinitarian God whose Son lived as Jesus of Nazareth and whose Spirit lives daily in human hearts. . . . This is not the God of Matthew Tindal and Thomas Paine, but rather their God who has since gotten a serious 'makeover' by Leo Buscaglia, Oprah Winfrey, and *Self* Magazine. Times change. So must God, it seems.[10]

This is a least-common-denominator religious faith but one that is particularly appropriate for an individualistic, consumer-oriented culture, driven by the advertising industry, liberal in its polity, and pluralistic. It "does not challenge the existent social, cultural, and political order, nor does it expect its adherents to do so."[11] But is it faith in the God of Abraham, Isaac, and Jacob? Is it the God of Jesus or of his church?

In an interesting theological comment, one worth our reflection, Smith accepts after some reluctance the thesis of Thomas Luckmann that mainstream American religions—including evangelical Protestantism—have undergone a process of *internal* secularization. According to Luckmann:

> Whereas religious ideas originally played an important part in the shaping of the American Dream, today the secular ideas of the American Dream pervade church religion. . . . [T]raditional church religion was pushed to the periphery of "modern" life in Europe while it became more "modern" in America by undergoing a process of internal secularization.[12]

Thus moralistic therapeutic deism, or whatever we want to call this contemporary, self-constructed faith, is not harmless. It is a rival religion, a cultural faith that is ultimately parasitic on historical religious traditions, draining away their life like remoras attached to sharks. Its very pervasiveness makes the transmission of historical religious faith all the more difficult. It is certainly not Christianity.[13] In our individualistic "culture of choice," even religion has become a commodity.[14]

What results is an image of a subjective God, privatized, secularized, unmediated by Scripture, Christian tradition, or church. It is not the God of

10. Ibid., 65.
11. Diane Winston, "Teach Your Children Well," in Heft, *Passing on the Faith,* 267.
12. Thomas Luckmann, *The Invisible Religion: The Problem of Religion in Modern Society* (New York: Macmillan, 1967) 36–37.
13. Smith, "Moralistic Therapeutic Deism," 66–68.
14. See, for example, Vincent J. Miller, *Consuming Religion: Christian Faith and Practice in a Consumer Culture* (New York: Continuum, 2004).

Israel or the God revealed in Jesus but one that is the product of popular culture. Traditional religious wisdom does not enter in. There is no sense of the incomprehensibility of the divine mystery, no search for a divine disclosure or self-revelation, no sense of a personal vocation. Thomas Merton, in an essay entitled "The Unbelief of Believers," long ago characterized such "believers" as uninterested in a God "who speaks or makes demands. . . . Their 'god' is simply an explanation and purification for the comfort and confusion of affluent society."[15]

The result is a comfortable, manageable, not very mysterious God, a God who makes no demands on the individual, who is "always there for me" or one who is "always looking out for me," a comforting and accepting presence rather than a God who challenges, forgives, and renews. In the Ignatian language of the Spiritual Exercises, it represents a claimed "experience" of God but one lacking the grace of the First Week, that profound sense that our sins have been forgiven and we are loved by a merciful God.

Counter Voices

Some religious sociologists are beginning to critique these uncritical concepts of spirituality so popular today. Robert Wuthnow, perhaps the premiere sociologist of religion in the U.S. today, is one of them. He writes, "The idea that spirituality is being pursued outside of organized religion is both plausible and worrisome."[16] He wonders how surveys can effectively measure people's interest in spirituality when spirituality itself can mean so many different things. Much of it seems irrational, based on self-indulgent fantasizing, or essentially private, personally invented sets of beliefs and practices. When books like *Chicken Soup for the Soul* and *The Celestine Prophecy* pass for spirituality, serious observers of American religion are concerned, "because they provide ready-made answers for the small setbacks and petty anxieties of ordinary life but do not speak of a righteous God who demands anything of believers."[17]

Wuthnow notes that among those who say that spirituality is fairly important, three-quarters do not attend religious services regularly and half are not church members. Thus questions could be raised about the seriousness of their spiritual commitment. He argues that "people with the highest commitment to spiritual

15. Thomas Merton, *Faith and Violence: Christian Teaching and Christian Practice* (Notre Dame, IN: University of Notre Dame Press, 1968) 201.

16. Robert Wuthnow, *All in Sync: How Music and Art Are Revitalizing American Religion* (Berkeley: University of California Press, 2003) 32.

17. Ibid., 24–25, at 25.

growth are overwhelmingly involved in religious organization: eighty percent of those who value spiritual growth the most are church members, and seventy-one percent say they attend worship services almost every week."[18] This tendency to identify spirituality with personal subjective feelings, without service of others or a community of faith that mediates the riches of a tradition or to whom one might be held accountable, is highly problematic.

In his book *Consuming Religion*, Vincent Miller warns that such spiritualities, shaped by the habits of our consumer-driven society, transform even the religious values we profess. Consumption becomes the dominant cultural practice, though he also points out that a consumer culture is experienced by many as liberating, allowing people to construct their own identities, freeing them from cultural constraints, external authorities, and predetermined gender and social roles.[19] This needs to be acknowledged.

Nevertheless, this "commodification" of religion itself is problematic. It reduces the riches of our religious traditions to images, symbols, music, paraphernalia, practices, and personalities that seekers can select from, and it deprives them of their ability to shape daily life. Like rosaries hanging from an automobile's rearview mirror but never prayed. Spirituality becomes disconnected from religion, while the "stuff" of religion, its appropriated symbols and practices, are separated from their original liturgical, communal, and institutional contexts. Religious traditions become repositories of interesting objects for personal choice. The result is privatization of religion,

> a dissolution of the coherence of religions reducing them to a palette of "cultural resources" that can be employed in any number of ways—even ways fundamentally at odds with the basic logic of their original religious tradition. This fragmentation also divorces faith from practice. Symbols, beliefs, and even spiritual disciplines become free-floating cultural objects ready to be put to whatever use we desire.[20]

This explains in part the popularity of Joseph Campbell, who has popularized and made widely available symbols and practices from the world religions, but stripped them from their communal and institutional contexts so that they can be appropriated by individuals into their own private religions or spiritualities. Some speak of this as the "deregulation" of religion, freeing it from the tradition in which it has been embedded and from its authority.[21]

---

18. Ibid., 36; Penny Marler and Kirk Hadaway reach a similar conclusion in "'Being Religious' or 'Being Spiritual in America,'" 297.

19. Miller, *Consuming Religion*, 225–28.

20. Ibid., 84.

21. See David Lyon, *Jesus in Disneyland: Religion in Postmodern Times* (Malden, MA: Blackwell, 2000).

While Miller does not see the deregulation of religion as necessarily negative or that spiritualities personally chosen, like commodities, are necessarily
shallow, he argues that spirituality needs communal support if it is to be more
than sentiment. When religious beliefs and practices are abstracted from the
cultures, institutions, and relationships in which they were once embedded,
they can no longer inform the shape of daily life: "Commitments to visions
of the spiritual life, no matter how profound, are difficult to sustain without
a community of shared belief. Furthermore, if religious syntheses are to inform the practice of daily life, they require some articulation in discipline
and practices. This again is difficult to achieve on the individual level."[22]

One way to counter the commodification of religion is to stress engagement in the liturgical, the sacramental, and the ecclesial. The church lives
from a tradition reaching back to the earliest Christian communities; it is
essentially public, not private. Sacraments are coded by that tradition. Scripture is read from a lectionary shared by the global church; it is not chosen
on the basis of personal preference. As Miller says, in the liturgy "one is not
free to yawn and move on to a more interesting passage, or to decide that it
is irrelevant."[23]

The "hookup" culture of our campuses today reflects this privatization
of religion, reducing it to a vague spirituality. Religion is separated from
life, and sex is separated from relationships. Christian faith emphasizes the
sanctity of the marital relationship and the integrity of the body, destined
for immortality (1 Cor 6:14). One young adult characterized the moral
consciousness of her peers as "if it makes me happy it's OK." Two recent
studies emphasize the deleterious effects of the separation of religion from
life. In her book, *Hooking Up*, Kathleen Bogle says that neither their religious affiliation nor their religious beliefs had a major effect on the participation in the hookup culture of the students she interviewed, including those
from Catholic colleges.[24] Donna Freitas, in *Sex and the Soul*, divides today's
college students into those at evangelical institutions who refuse to separate
sex from religion and those at the "spiritual colleges," both public and private, including Catholic colleges, many of whom do. Virtually all the students
at the evangelical colleges spoke of their campus experience as explicitly
Christian, while for those at the Catholic schools she visited, Catholicism
seems to play almost no role in their studies or their relationships.[25]

22. Miller, *Consuming Religion*, 106.
23. Ibid., 202.
24. Kathleen A. Bogle, *Hooking Up: Sex, Dating, and Relationships on Campus* (New
York: New York University Press, 2008) 160.
25. Donna Freitas, *Sex and the Soul: Juggling Sexuality, Spirituality, Romance, and Religion on America's College Campuses* (New York: Oxford University Press, 2008) 65–70.

Freitas argues that the "spiritual but not religious" students are typically sexually active, but "because their spirituality is amorphous and ill defined, it does little to guide their sexual decision making."[26] At the end of her study, she lists four basic benefits lost by those who collectively turn away from their religious and spiritual traditions: boundaries, including limits and gradations of what is and is not permissible; a sense of right and wrong that is more than personal; a framework for discernment; and a sense for forgiveness and redemption that comes ultimately from God.[27]

Beyond a Culturally Determined Faith

So how can we help our young people have that "burning bush" experience (Exod 3:2) that so transformed Moses? How can we as Catholic ministers and educators help them, many of whom are drawn to service, move beyond the self-chosen, culturally determined faiths and spiritualities of *Chicken Soup for the Soul* and discover the face of Jesus? How can we help them experience the God who awakens their generosity? God of course remains mystery. We cannot engineer such an encounter, so that it happens in a place we have chosen or according to a schedule we have determined. We can only be witnesses, mediators, and fellow pilgrims. But there are things we can do.

First, be honest. Be suspicious of substitutes. And be yourself, willing to share your own experience. Personal witness or testimony is important to young people. Pope Paul VI was well aware of this. In his great apostolic exhortation on evangelization, *Evangelii nuntiandi* (no. 41), he wrote: "Modern man listens more willingly to witnesses than to teachers, and if he does listen to teachers, it is because they are witnesses." Andrew Greeley continually reminds us that the tradition of the church, what he likes to call our "Catholic religious sensibility," is passed on first of all by parents and spouses and by telling stories.[28] He likes to contrast the popular tradition, the Catholicism you learned before you went to school, with what he calls the high tradition, contained in the teaching of theologians and the magisterium.[29] We need to be willing to tell our own stories and those of our mentors in the faith.

Second, we need to address these issues of faith and theology in a nonthreatening, nonjudgmental way. Part of the relativism of contemporary

26. Ibid., 221.
27. Ibid., 227.
28. Andrew Greeley, *The Catholic Imagination* (Los Angeles: University of California Press, 2000) 175.
29. Ibid., 76.

culture as well as the pluralism and celebration of diversity that characterizes higher education is an allergic reaction to anything that sounds judgmental. How can one religious view be better than another? Aren't they all good? Can't they all be true? So tolerance becomes the highest virtue. From a slightly different perspective, Cardinal Carlo Martini characterizes the post-modern mentality as preferring beauty to truth. "There is acceptance of every form of dialogue and exchange because of a desire to be always open to another and to what is different."[30] What gets lost with our postmodernist ethos is the very possibility of truth.

How do we help those working with young people today address the relativism of contemporary, postmodern culture? John Cusick speaks of the need for a "new apologetics" for young adults that will require parish ministry leaders to learn their language and use the media that they use. He cites two successful Catholic web sites targeting young adults—his own Young Adult Ministry and Busted Halo, and I might also add the Young Life web site and Sacred Space, a web site operated by the Irish Jesuits.[31] I would rather speak of a new catechesis, an instruction or spiritual direction that is honest and real but also rooted in experience.

Third, we need to move from an informational or content-based model of catechesis to one that integrates witness, experience, and the actual practice of the church, so that the whole church, not just the specialists, has the responsibility for catechesis. This was stressed repeatedly by the contributors to Robert Imbelli's fine volume *Handing on the Faith*.[32] This is especially important for students in Catholic colleges and universities. How do we expand the classroom experience so that it embraces the world as it is today, bringing the poor, the disadvantaged, the suffering into the conversation that good teaching should facilitate? How do we create learning communities which can help our students move beyond the superficiality of contemporary culture and engage with fundamental issues of faith?

To answer these questions we have considered community-based or service learning classes or church-related study abroad programs that give our students direct contact with the poor. Such educational experiences are powerful for many students; they touch their hearts, helping them to see the proclamation of the kingdom of God as the true mission of the church. They

---

30. Carlo Maria Martini, "Teach the Faith in a Postmodern World," *America* 198/16 (2008) 18.

31. See www.yamchicago.com; www.bustedhalo.com; www.younglife.org; and www.sacredspace.ie.

32. See the chapters by Paul Griffith, Christopher and Deborah Ruddy, Terrence Tilley, Thomas Groome, and Blaise Cupich in *Handing on the Faith: The Church's Mission and Challenge*, ed. Robert P. Imbelli (New York: Crossroad, 2006).

are educational experiences that are truly transformative. We need more opportunities for such classes but that will mean a commitment to raising the necessary funds, grants for faculty development of integrative courses, and endowments to fund immersion programs as well as the centers to support them.

Fourth, I think we need to take more seriously Pope Benedict's call for a deeper sense of being in the presence of the holy, particularly for a greater reverence in the liturgy. I must admit that I find much of his writing on the liturgy one-sided, with his preference for a more formal, priest-centered liturgy with the congregation kneeling, his concern to emphasize the differences between the ordained and the nonordained as well as his views on facing east, inclusive language, creativity, dancing—all suggesting a much more traditional approach to liturgy.[33]

At the same time, his calls for greater reverence and more silence in the liturgy are well taken. An overemphasis on the Eucharist as a communal, "festive" meal has led to a loss of its sacred and sacrificial dimensions. If the liturgical experimentation of the 70s and early 80s is behind us, the language of lectors and presiders at least in the United States too often focuses on celebration, community, ministry, and hospitality, with far less attention to entering into the holy or approaching the altar of God.

Too often our liturgies have become overly wordy, didactic, and even banal. Those coming from a highly sensate culture, overstimulated, constantly talking or texting on cell phones, choosing from the hundreds of songs on their iPods, or from a world of images only a mouse click away, are accustomed to being in control. As someone has said, "If you have an iPod, you don't need to listen to any song you don't love." Thus many from this generation have lost a sense for worship. They tire easily of repeated liturgical formulas and familiar eucharistic prayers. Ritual no longer satisfies; they want variety. As Ratzinger has written:

> This is why, here especially, we are in such urgent need of an education toward inwardness. We need to be taught to enter into the heart of things. As far as liturgy is concerned, this is a matter of life or death. The only way we can be saved from succumbing to the inflation of words is if we have the courage to face silence and in it learn to listen afresh to *the Word*. Otherwise we shall be overwhelmed by "mere words" at the very point where we should be encountering the Word, the Logos, the Word of love, crucified and risen, who brings us life and joy.[34]

---

33. See Joseph Ratzinger, *The Spirit of the Liturgy* (San Francisco: Ignatius Press, 2000).

34. Joseph Ratzinger, *Feast of Faith: Approaches to a Theology of the Liturgy* (San Francisco: Ignatius Press, 1986) 73.

Finally, we need to encourage young people to become comfortable with prayer and retreat experiences which privilege silence. The extroversion of contemporary life, with music, television, and the constant intrusiveness of the advertising industry, leaves little room for silence. Young people especially are surrounded by electronically mediated conversations, sounds, and images. Stimulation is constant. On campus I watch students walking alone but always talking on cell phones. Dominican University's William George calls for a greater emphasis on solitude in undergraduate education.[35] Similarly, Cardinal Martini has written, "We need to move away from an unhealthy slavery to rumors and endless chattering, from characterless music that only makes noise, and find each day at least one half-hour of silence and a half-day each week to think about ourselves, to reflect and pray for a longer period."[36]

For it is in silence that we encounter the mysterious divine presence. As Meister Eckhart says, "Nothing in all creation is so like God as stillness." It is interesting that some contemporary contemplative communities, already committed to long periods of silence, schedule weekly "desert days" for their members so that, freed from normal routines, they can experience an even greater solitude and silence.

God speaks in silence. God's presence is beyond image and word. It is comforting, sustaining, life-giving. It brings a deep sense of peace. We know that we have been touched, that we are not alone.

Conclusion

According to Robert Wuthnow, the one word that best describes young adults' approach to religion and spirituality is "tinkering," choosing from resources and materials readily at hand.[37] With religion so often reduced to one more commodity to be consumed, the task for those who take religion seriously is to rediscover its ability to convey a conception of self and society that is an alternative to the one imposed by the market. Jack Miles sees young people as longing for authenticity. Using Taizé as one of his examples, he concludes: "Religious institutions, even making the most active use of showbiz techniques, cannot possibly compete in that game. But mystery is their

35. William P. George, "Learning Alone," *America* 199/7 (2008) 16.
36. Martini, "Teach the Faith," 20.
37. Rubert Wuthnow, *After the Baby Boomers: How Twenty- and Thirty-Somethings Are Shaping the Future of American Religion* (Princeton, NJ: Princeton University Press, 2007) 13–15.

own game, and perhaps they need to return to it."[38] The fact that some sociologists of religion are beginning to challenge the divorce of spirituality from religion is encouraging.

Our Catholic tradition has many treasures in its rich and diverse heritage, for example, the legacy of St. Anthony and the early desert *abbas* and *ammas* which continues in the monastic life today, the nature mysticism of Francis of Assisi and his devotion to the poor, the Rhineland mystics of the thirteen century, the "contemplative in action" spirituality of Ignatius Loyola, the bridal mysticism of Teresa of Avila, the mysticism of the dark night of John of the Cross in the sixteenth century, the practical spirituality of Francis de Sales in the seventeenth, and the communities of women religious in the nineteenth century who dedicated themselves to various works of charity, including care for the poor and suffering, education and hospital work and other ministries for the needy.

The twentieth century has seen a multitude of new communities and spiritualities, from the different families that trace their inspiration to Charles de Foucauld (1858–1916), Catholic Worker (1933) and L'Arche (1964) communities founded on the Beatitudes, to the new ecclesial movements such as Opus Dei (1928), Focolari (1943), Communion and Liberation (1954), Marriage Encounter (1962), the Charismatic Renewal (1967), Sant'Egidio (1968), and the Neocatechumenal Way (late 60s).

What all these communities have in common, in spite of their great diversity, is that they make possible for their members an encounter with God in Christ, mediated by Word, sacrament, and the community of the church. This is how Joseph Ratzinger, now Pope Benedict XVI, understands conversion in its full New Testament sense. He argues that conversion always comes from the Lord through the church; a person cannot accomplish it alone: "One does not simply confer faith upon oneself. By its very nature, faith is always the establishment of fellowship with all the brethren of Jesus in his holy Church, from which alone it can be received."[39] Elsewhere he describes conversion as an encounter with the Word which effects a change from the subjective "I" to the "we of the Church."[40]

---

38. Jack Miles, "The Leisure of Worship and the Worship of Leisure," in Heft, *Passing on the Faith,* 263.

39. Joseph Ratzinger, *Principles of Catholic Theology: Building Stones for a Fundamental Theology* (San Francisco: Ignatius Press, 1987) 34; Vincent Twomey discusses Ratzinger's understanding of conscience in *Pope Benedict XVI: The Conscience of Our Age* (San Francisco: Ignatius Press, 2007) 121–34.

40. Joseph Ratzinger, *The Nature and Mission of Theology* (San Francisco: Ignatius Press, 1995) 58–61.

This is a difficult teaching for many members of an individualistic generation, so accustomed to disconnecting spirituality from religion and comfortable with images of God constructed from popular culture rather than Christian faith. We owe them much more.

Contributors

Don J. Briel, doctorate in theology from the University of Strasbourg, is the Koch Chair in Catholic Studies and director of the Center for Catholic Studies at the University of St. Thomas in St. Paul, Minnesota. Specializing in Newman studies, ecclesiology, and dogmatic theology, he also serves on the advisory boards of the Lumen Christi Institute at the University of Chicago and the Center for Ethics and Culture at the University of Notre Dame.

David Gentry-Akin, Ph.D. and S.T.D from the Catholic University of Louvain, is professor of theology at Saint Mary's College of California in Moraga. A specialist in foundational theology, he has become increasingly interested in recent years in the question of mission and identity in Catholic institutions and the contribution that theologians can make to that effort.

Kristin E. Heyer, Ph.D. from Boston College, is an associate professor in the department of religious studies at Santa Clara University. She taught Christian ethics for six years at Loyola Marymount University prior to her present position, including courses on Catholic social thought and HIV/AIDS.

Stephen J. Pope, professor of social ethics in the theology department of Boston College, received his Ph.D. in theological ethics from the University of Chicago. He has written *The Evolution of Altruism and the Ordering of Love* (Georgetown, 1994) and *Human Evolution and Christian Ethics* (Cambridge, 2007), and edited *Essays on the Ethics of St. Thomas Aquinas* (Georgetown, 2002) as well as articles on the virtue of charity, social justice, natural law and human rights, and political forgiveness.

Thomas P. Rausch, S.J., Ph.D. from Duke University, is the T. Marie Chilton Professor of Catholic Theology at Loyola Marymount University in Los Angeles. Teaching in the areas of ecclesiology, Christology, and ecumenism, he served on the Catholic/Southern Baptist Conversation (1994–2001) and the Catholic/World Evangelical Alliance Consultation (2001–03). He is a member of the Anglican/Roman Catholic Consultation USA, cochairs the Los Angeles Catholic/Evangelical Committee and the Theological Commission for the Archdiocese of Los Angeles.

Mark Ravizza, S.J., received his Ph.D. from Yale University. He is associate professor of philosophy and a senior fellow of the Bannan Institute for Jesuit Education at Santa Clara University. He is currently teaching in El Salvador at the Casa de la Solidaridad, a study abroad program sponsored by Santa Clara University.

Index

Abbott, Walter, 40, 104
abortion, 19, 53
Ackeren, Gerald van, 16
Acosta, José de, 8
Aeterni Patris, 24
AIDS, 51, 104, 106, 109, 120
AJCU, 70
Albert the Great, 20
Alexander of Hales, 20
Alwin, Alice, 71
American Catholic Philosophical
    Association, 14
American Catholics Today, 59–60, 64,
    67
Angelicum, 87
Antony, St., 155
Aquinas, Thomas, 21, 22, 23, 34
L'Arche, 155
Aristotle, 7
Arrupe, Pedro, xiii, 43–47, 138
Astin, Alexander, 144
Augustine, 15, 20, 34

Baier, Annette, 114
Balasuriya, Tissa, 30
Bangert, William, 8, 10
Baró, Martín, 49
Basil, Council of, 22
Beaudoin, Tom, 63
Beirne, Charles, 48–49
Benedict XVI, Pope, 2–3, 30, 101–2,
    139, 143, 152, 153

Bible, 24, 25
Black, Christopher, 9
Boff, Leonardo, 30
Bogle, Kathleen, 150
Bonaventure, 20, 23
Borgia, Francis, 5
Boston College, 15, 55, 70, 107, 127,
    135
Brackley, Dean, 47, 52–54, 106, 107,
    133
Briel, Don, xiii, 76
Brockey, Liam, 7
Buckley, Michael, 5, 21, 112
Burgaleta, Claudio, 8
Burke, Kevin, 48–49
Burleigh, Michael, 76
Burtchaell, James, 15
Byrne, Patrick, 107

Call to Action, 61
Campbell, Joseph, 149
Campion, Edmund, 10
campus ministry, 17, 28, 36
Canisius, Peter, 10
Carey, Patrick, 13, 15, 27, 28, 32
Casa de la Solidaridad, xiv, 70, 112
Catholic Church, 60–61, 99
Catholic colleges and universities, xii,
    1–19, 47–57, 78, 83, 133, 150–52
    Catholic identity, 2, 14–19, 30–31,
        37, 90
    Jesuit, 3–12, 20, 112

in the U.S., 1, 12, 18
professionalization of, xii, 1–2, 32
Catholic social doctrine, 40–57
Catholic Studies, 76–91
Catholic Theological Society of
    America, 28, 29
Catholic University of America, 15, 17,
    26, 143
Catholic web sites, 152
Catholic Worker, 155
Catholics, American, 59–60, 64
    Hispanic, 62, 88
Catholics, young adult, xii, 38, 58–75,
    92–94, 143–56
    and ministry, 63, 65, 69
    institutional commitment, 60, 64, 74
    religious literacy, xii, 62–63, 73–74,
        83
    sexual attitudes, 60, 61, 65, 74, 137,
        150–51
Centesimus annus, 43
Chapple, Christopher, 20, 57
Chardin, Teilhard de, 26
Chenu, Marie-Dominique, 23, 26
Chesterton, G. K., 26
Christian Brothers, xi, 12, 95
Christian Life Communities, 11, 67
Christic imagination, xiv, 123–25
Christo Rey schools, xi, 89
church, 39–40, 43, 44, 152
Clavius, Christopher, 8
Coleman, John, 145
College Theology Society, 28
Communion and Liberation, 155
communities, new, 155
community-based learning, 103–10
confraternities, 9
Congar, Yves, 22, 26
Congregation for the Doctrine of the
    Faith, 29, 30, 52
Constance, Council of, 22
Cooke, Bernard, 27, 28
Cooper, John, 15
Coster, Francis, 10

Crowley, Paul, 19, 57
crucified people, 48, 50, 52
culture of choice, 38, 62, 147
Cunningham, Lawrence, 20–21, 32–34
cura personalis, 9, 56
    and spiritual formation, 9
Curran, Charles, 22, 29, 30
curriculum, 11, 14, 17, 33, 36, 141
Curtiss, Eldon, 31
Cusick, John, 61, 152

Danner, Mark, 131
D'Antonio, William, 58, 62, 64, 67,
    68, 73
Darcy, John, 19
Davidson, James, 60, 73
Dawson, Christopher, 77, 78
Day, Dorothy, 34
deism, 146
Denton, Melinda, 59, 145
Devine, Richard, 69
Diekmann, Godfrey, 17
Dillard, Annie, 126
Dinges, William, 60, 73
dissent, 30
Divino afflante Spiritu, 25
"Doctrinal Responsibility," 29
Dominicans, 9, 12
drama and the arts, 8, 10
Drey, Sebastian von, 24
Dulles, Avery, 22
Dupuis, Jacques, 30

Ebeling, Gerhard, 24
Ecclesia in America, 135
"Ecclesial Vocation of the Theologian,"
    29
Eck, Johannes, 4
Eckhart, Meister, 20, 154
Ellacuría, Ignacio, 47–50
Elliot, Larry, 130
Ellis, John Tracy, 17
El Mazote, 131
eloquentia perfecta, 7–8

eucharistic adoration, 72, 93
evangelical institutions, 150
Evangelii nuntiandi, 43, 151
Ex corde ecclesiae, 30–31, 79–80, 127
experience, importance of, 66–68, 113

Facebook, 65, 68
faith, 66, 73, 92–94, 125, 143, 145–48,
   155
   and justice, 38, 39–57, 128
   and reason, 23, 92
   faith that does justice, xii, 45–46, 57
Farmer, Paul, 130
Favre, Pierre, 4, 9
Fenton, Joseph, 25–26
Fitzgerald, Paul, 54–55
Flannery, Austin, 40, 142
Florence, Council of, 22
Flynn, Maureen, 9
Focolari, 155
Ford, Ita, 53
Foucauld, Charles de, 155
Francis of Assisi, 155
Franciscans, 9, 12
freedom of inquiry, 42
Freitas, Donna, 65, 150–51
Freux, André des, 11

Gaillardetz, Richard, 29, 30
Gallagher, Eugene, 16
Gallagher, Raphael, 106
Ganss, George, 6, 12
Garraghan, Gilbert, 12
Gaudium et spes, 39–42
GC 35, 104
Gebara, Ivone, 30
Gentry-Akin, David, xiii, 92
George, Cardinal Francis, 76
George, William, 154
Georgetown University, 13, 15
Gerson, Jean, 20
Gillis, Chester, 35–36
Gilpatrick, Breanne, 130
Gilson, Étienne, 14

Gleason, Philip, 2, 13–16, 26
God, image of, 144–48
   speaks in silence, 154
Goizueta, Roberto, 55, 68
Gonzaga University, 15, 55
Good Shepherd Volunteers, 69
Gössmann, Elisabeth, 27
Gragnani, Vincent, 69
Gray, Mark, 61
Greeley, Andrew, 73, 151
Gregorian University, 7
Gregory XIII, Pope, 10
Griffith, Paul, 152
Groome, Thomas, 152
Gutiérrez, Gustavo, 30, 55, 68, 128

Haight, Roger, 25, 30
Harris, Joseph, 61
Harvard University, 13
Hastings, Adrian, 39
Hatcher, Julie, 69
Hauerwas, Stanley, 68
Haughey, John, 34–35
Hayes, Mike, 93
Hebblethwaite, Peter, 39
Heft, James, 32–33, 35, 66, 73
Hesburgh, Theodore, 1, 18, 19
Heyer, Kristin, xiii, 103
Hinsdale, Mary Ann, 81
Hinze, Bradford, 30
hiring for mission, 36
Hiroshima, 43–44
Hoge, Dean, 60, 68, 73
Hollenbach, David, 136
Holy Cross Associates, 69
homosexuality, 61, 65
hookup culture, 150–51
Horan, Michael, 65
Huesman, William, 16
Humani generis, 25
humanities, 6–7

Ignatius of Loyola, 3, 11, 20–21, 46,
   66, 155

Imbelli, Robert, 66, 152
immersion trips, 70, 127–42
immigration, 41, 105, 108
Index, 24
"Instruction on the Ecclesial Vocation
    of the Theologian," 29
interdisciplinary approach, 81, 83–86
interreligious dialogue, 57

Jay, Claude, 4
Jenkins, Philip, 66
Jesuit education, 6–9, 44, 46
Jesuit Educational Association, 14
Jesuit Educational Quarterly, 16
Jesuit Volunteer Corps, 69, 140
Jesuits, xii, 3–12
    colleges and universities, 3–12, 21,
        44–45, 47–54
    Constitutions, 3, 9, 11, 20, 21,
    famous graduates, 12
    founded, 3
    suppression of, 12
Jesus, 56, 138, 143, 151
Jesus Seminar, 36
Jewell, Marti, 68
John of the Cross, 155
John Paul II, Pope, 30, 43, 79, 82, 127,
    135–36 143
John XXIII, Pope, 26, 39

Kearney, G. R., xii
Kieslowski, Krzysztof, 118
Kircher, Athanasius, 8
Kolvenbach, Peter-Hans, xiv, 55–56,
    103, 111, 113, 115, 126, 127, 128
Küng, Hans, 17

Laínez, Diego, 4, 5
Lamentabili sane, 25
Land O'Lakes, 1, 82, 91
Landy, Thomas, 90
Lasalle-Klein, Robert, 48–49
Lay Centre Foyer Unitas, 94
Lazarus, Francis, 112
Leahy, William, 1, 14, 16

Lee, Bernard, 67
Leo XIII, Pope, 24
Lerner, Melvin, 136
Lernoux, Penny, 47
Leunis, Jean, 9
Lewis, Harry, 76–77, 78
L'Heureux, John, 122
Liber sententiarum, 21
liturgy, 63, 71–72, 150, 153
Loewe, William, 52
Lombard, Peter, 21
Lonergan, Bernard, 25
Loyola Marymount University, 32, 70,
    104
Loyola University of Chicago, 18
Lubac, Henri de, 26
Luckmann, Thomas, 147
Lynch, William, 122–25
Lyon, David, 149
Lyons, Council of, 22

Mack, Burton, 36
magisterium, 21–22, 24, 25, 29–30, 151
Mahoney, Kathleen, 13–14
mandatum, 30–31
Marcel, Gabriel, 118–19
Marian congregations, 9–11
Maritan, Jacques, 14
Marler, Penny, 145, 149
Marquette University, 18, 27
Marriage Encounter, 155
Marsden, George, 38
Martini, Cardinal Carlo, 152, 153
Maryknoll Lay Volunteers, 69
Mayorga, Román, 48
McBrien, Richard, 35
McCool, Gerald, 24, 25
McDonagh, Enda, 42, 106
McDonald, William, 17
McEnroy, Carmel, 30
McKenzie, John, 26
Mediator Dei, 25
men and women for others, 44–45, 56,
    138

Mendes, Sam, 117
Merton, Thomas, 148
Milanovic, Branko, 130
Miles, Jack, 72, 153
Millennials, 74, 93
Miller, Jerome, 121–22
Miller, Vincent, 68, 72, 147–50
Minnich, Nelson, 22
modernism, 25
modus parisiensis, 7–8, 11, 20
Möhler, Johann, 24
Mola, Yolanda de, 43
Moltmann, Jürgen, 50
monasticism, 155
   monastic theology, 22
Montes, Segundo, 49
Moralistic Therapeutic Deism, 145–47
Morey, Melanie, 14, 33, 56
Morris, Charles, 64
Mueller, J.J., 95
Muldoon, Tim, 58, 62–63, 65, 68, 71, 72
Murray, John Courtney, 16, 17, 26
Mystici corporis, 25

Nadal, Jerome, 5
Napoleon, 76
NativityMiguel schools, xi
Neocatechumenal Way, 155
Neo-Scholasticism, 2, 14–15, 17
Newman, John, 24, 47, 50, 80–81
Nobili, Roberto de, 8
Nolan, Albert, 132
Notre Dame, 18, 19, 55

Obama, Barack, 19
O'Brien, David, 2, 90–91
O'Dea, Thomas, 17
O'Malley, John, 3–6, 8–11
O'Meara, Thomas, 32
O'Neill, William, 55
option for the poor, 48, 51
Opus Dei, 155
Orsuto, Donna, 94
Orwell, George, 129

Padberg, John, 3, 20
Palmer, Parker, 118
Pascendi dominici gregis, 25
Paul III, Pope, 3, 5, 24
Paul VI, Pope, 43, 151
Paulussen, Louis, 10
Pavur, Claude, 11
Pelikan, Jaroslav, 143
Pentecostalism, 66
Pew Forum Survey 2008, 61, 144
Phan, Peter, 30
philosophy, 14–17
Piderit, John, 14, 33, 56
Pius X, Pope, 25
Pius XII, Pope, 25
Poblete, Renato, 66
Polanco, Juan de, 11
poor, the, 8, 39, 41–42, 45, 50–52, 130, 135, 138–39
Pope, Stephen, xiv, 127, 138
Populorum progressio, 44
Portier, William, 61
praxis-based education, 111–26
Protestant colleges, 13, 37–38
proyección social, 47–50, 54
PULSE program, 55, 107

Quinn, John, 19

Rahner, Karl, 26, 47, 117
Ramirez, Margaret, 61
Ratio studiorum, 11
Ratzinger, Joseph, 30, 42, 153; *see also* Benedict XVI
Rausch, Thomas, xii, 60, 67, 72, 100
Ravizza, Mark, xiv, 111
Reese, Thomas, 61
Reformers, 23–24
Regina Mundi, 27
religion, 147, 148–50
religious studies, 27, 28, 32–33
ressourcement, 25
Rhineland mystics, 155
Ricci, Mateo, 8
Richardson, Cyril, 95

Rogers, Rosemary, 28
Roman curia, 25
Romero, Oscar, 48
Ruddy, Christopher, 37, 152
Ruddy, Debora, 152
Ryan, Robin, 65

Saint Mary's College, 94, 102
Sales, Francis de, 10
Sant'Egidio, 87, 98, 155
Santa Clara University, 49, 111–12
Schillebeeckx, Edward, 51
Schneiders, Sandra, 24
scholastics, 4, 7, 15
School of the Americas, 46–47, 56
Seattle University, 18
Second Vatican Council, 38–42
Seiger of Brabant, 20
service learning, 54, 69; *see also*
    community-based learning
Sheed, Frank, 26
Sikora, Jennifer, 18
Sisters of Mercy, 12
Smith, Christian, 59, 73, 145
Sobrino, Jon, 30, 47, 50–52, 138
sodalities, 9–10
solidarity, 56, 111, 113, 115, 127, 133,
    135, 140
Sommerville, C., 77
Soul Searching, 59, 145–46
Spiritual Exercises, 3, 9, 21, 50, 66,
    148
spiritual, not religious, 143–45,
    148–51, 155
spirituality, xiv, 45, 68, 138, 143–49,
    151
"Spirituality in Higher Education,"
    UCLA study, 144–45
Steinfels, Peter, 36–37
Summa theologiae, 21
Synod of Bishops, 1971, 42

Taizé, 71, 72, 153
Taylor, Charles, 73, 144
Teresa of Avila, 155

theology, theologians, xii, 6, 15–17,
    20–38
    and councils, 22
    and faith formation, 28, 35–38
    and Reformers, 24
    as architectonic wisdom, 21, 23
    in Middle Ages, xii, 21–22
    laicization of, 26, 28–29
    liberation, 45, 47–52, 141
    Roman, 24–25
    undergraduate, 15–17, 32–38
    women in, 27
"Theses on the Relationship between
    the Ecclesial Magisterium and
    Theology," 29
Thijssen, J., 22
Tilley, Terrence, 68, 152
"To Defend the Faith," 30–31
Tracy, David, 26, 34
Traub, George, 111
Trent, Council of, 7, 22
truth, 152
Tübingen School, 24

universities, 1–19
    and moral authority, 77–78
    medieval, 6, 20
University of Central America, xiii,
    46–52
University of Paris, 20, 22
University of St. Thomas, 81–91

van Engen, Jo Ann, 132
Vatican II, 15, 17, 26, 39–42
Vienne, Council of, 22
Villaret, Emile, 10

Weigel, Gustave, 17
White, Robert, 94
Wilcox, John, 90
Wilkin, Robert, 73
Winston, Diane, 147
Wister, Robert, 16
Wolff, Sr. M., 27
women, 27, 41, 141

Woods, Thomas, 95
Wuthnow, Robert, 58, 148, 153

"Young Adult Catholics and their
    Future in Ministry," 63, 69

young adults, *see* Catholics, young
    adults

Zilbauer, Brian, 145
Zubiri, Xavier, 47–48